SANKOFA

STORIES OF POWER, HOPE, AND JOY

JAWANZA KUNJUFU

Chicago, Illinois

Front Cover illustration by Tony Quaid
Copyright © 1998 by Jawanza Kunjufu
First Edition, First Printing

All scriptural references are from the
New King James Bible.

Contents

Foreword

I have become fascinated by the power of stories. People who cannot remember the major points in a speech or sermon will however, remember the stories almost verbatim. We usually think that stories are for children. The reality is that stories are beneficial for everyone. I have loved reading about the great African writer Aesop.

I have had the privilege of being pastored for more than two decades by Jeremiah Wright, Jr., who is one of the best storytellers in America. Other great storytellers whom I've enjoyed over the years are the late Dr. Samuel Proctor, Gardner Taylor, John Bryant, Walter Thomas, Frederick Haynes III, and Ozzie Smith. The list of African American storytellers is endless because in a way, we are all storytellers.

In the spirit of the African storyteller Aesop, I have compiled the stories in this book to teach and transmit power, hope, and joy. Also, as a speaker and a lover of the Word, I wanted to collect all of my favorite stories in one volume.

Some of the stories you have read or heard before. Every attempt has been made to try to give credit to the original source for the story. The majority of the stories are historical and part of the public domain. If you are aware of other versions of the stories included in Sankofa, please forward to me at African American Images. If the Lord leads us to write a second volume, we would love to include your story. Please provide the original source.

Overview

Part One
(THE GREATEST STORYTELLER)

Part One of the book contains stories from the greatest Storyteller of them all: Jesus. These biblical stories set the tone for the entire book. My Lord and Savior taught in parables and this method has greatly influenced my own teaching style.

Part Two
(SANKOFA)

Part Two looks at the African experience from an African frame of reference, starting with the pyramids, going through the door of no return, and achieving emancipation and ultimately our quest for freedom.

Part Three
(POWER)

The insatiable desire of men and women who would not be defeated and had the will to win at any cost summarizes what these remarkable stories are all about.

Part Four
(HOPE AND JOY)

The following chapter is Hope and Joy. The media would have us believe that only bleak things happen in the African American community. The stories in this section describe how we are able to sing a song in Zion and continue to laugh and smile.

Part Five
(FAMILY)

Some of the best storytellers in the country just happen to be fathers and mothers. The stories reflect the beauty and challenges of family life.

Part Six
(NGUZO SABA AND MAAT)

These stories are entertaining and they teach the significance of morals, values, and ethics.

Part Seven
(COLLEGE)

I was pleasantly surprised that I had enough stories on collegiate experiences. This section is reserved just for college stories.

Part Eight
(NATURE)

Aesop's fables remind us of the beauty and power of nature and the lessons it can teach us if we are only willing to listen. We have become such a fast paced society that we can go the entire day and not hear the singing of the birds. These stories encourage us to slow down and learn from Nature.

Part Nine
(BIBLICAL STORIES)

It is not an accident that the book begins with Jesus Christ and ends with the power of His Word.

I speak to groups across the country, and whenever I am introduced as the author of *Hip Hop vs. Maat*, 90 percent of the time the word "Maat" is mispronounced, and probably misunderstood. I pray that the same thing does not happen with this book and the word "Sankofa." Because the movie by the same name was not distributed by a major Hollywood company, many African Americans did not see the film. Sankofa is a mythical bird in the Akan Ghanaian West African community that symbolizes the need to look back, to appreciate and learn from the past, in order to go forward.

Let us go back and enjoy our Lord and culture and then go out into the world and make it a better place.

Dedication

My sister and I celebrated the homegoing of our mother Mary Brown October 31, 1998. She was a fantastic mother. The poem below is written by my sister Cynthia Mayes.

Mom, the Wind is Blowing©

The feelings of today, are very new within my heart, I know as time proceeds, my ache will be set apart.
But as for here and now, I can only start to reflect. . . on the memories of the good times, that we shared as a set. . .
A mother and a daughter, neither really knowing what to do. . .
A series of trials and errors in the process of acquiring a clue.
A time of building a relationship, that was strong and unified,
A relationship of love and honor, that will never subside.
A time of celebrations, family dinners and the such,
A time of shopping endlessly and sharing a bit of lunch. . .
A time with words of encouragement, and support which had no bounds,
A time spent on caring and sharing, in the multitude of life's unexpected rounds.
My mom jokingly would always ask, if the "Wind was blowing". . .
I feel. . .
God blew the breath of life on my mom, and this year He took it back. . . .
He has the power to control the winds of life, least we not forget,
Let us not get so engrossed and pompous that we think we run the show,
That we have a say in this universal plan, that's so awesome, we dare not know. . . .
So when you see a sunset, and you feel a gentle breeze, be thankful for the moment, be thankful for your family, and never forget to tell them, that you love them.
My mom knew I loved her, and for that "I'm Thankful."

God Bless!

PART 1

THE GREATEST STORYTELLER

"But without a parable He did not speak to them. And when they were alone, He explained all things to His disciples."

Mark 4:34

One Solitary Life

He was born in an obscure village, the child of a peasant woman. He grew up in still another village, where he worked in a carpenter shop until he was 30. Then for three years he was an itinerant preacher.

He never wrote a book.

He never held an office.

He never had a family or owned a house.

He didn't go to college.

He never traveled 200 miles from the place where he was born.

He did none of these things one usually associates with greatness.

He had no credentials but himself.

He was only 33 when public opinion turned against him. His friends ran away. He was turned over to his enemies and went through the mockery of a trial. He was nailed to a cross between two thieves.

When he was dying, his executioners gambled for his clothing, the only property he had on earth. When he was dead, he was laid in a borrowed grave through the pity of a friend.

Nineteen centuries have come and gone, and today he is the central figure of the human race, the leader of mankind's progress.

All the armies that ever marched, all the navies that ever sailed, all the parliaments that ever sat, all the kings that ever reigned, put together, have not affected the life of man on earth as much as that One Solitary Life.

Anonymous

The Sower of Seeds

Behold, a sower went out to sow.

And as he sowed, some seed fell by the wayside; and the birds came and devoured them.

Some fell on stony places, where they did not have much earth: and they immediately sprang up because they had no depth of earth.

But when the sun was up they were scorched, and because they had no root they withered away.

And some fell among thorns, and the thorns sprang up and choked them.

But others fell on good ground and yielded a crop: some a hundredfold, some sixty, some thirty.

He who has ears to hear, let him hear!

Matthew 13:3-8

This is one of my favorite stories. Jesus is teaching that the seed is the Word. Many of us are in church listening to the Word, and before we can leave the sanctuary the devil has taken the Word from us. I often ask people after church what was the sermon about? Five minutes after the benediction, they are unable to answer. While they were listening to the sermon, they were thinking about what they were going to make for dinner, or their dinner reservations, who is winning the game or a litany of other plans for the day. Others were more involved in what people around them were wearing. Jesus reminds us that for many of us, the Word is taken before we leave the sanctuary.

When the Word falls on "stony places," that means that we have not absorbed the Word into our hearts, minds, and souls. Many church members do not take their Bibles to church and don't read the Bible and pray during the week, therefore, the Word is not nurtured and does not grow. There are Christians who were saved decades ago but remain at the same spiritual level.

What are the thorns that choke out the Word? Today's thorns are called Visa, MasterCard, American Express, Lexus, Mercedes, BMW, television, sports, gambling, careers, graduate degrees, and whatever else takes our minds off Him.

Jesus always leaves us with good news. From now on, when you hear the Word, take it home with you. Water and nurture it by reading more Word. Pray, meditate, fellowship with other believers, and stand on the Word, and it will grow a hundredfold.

Talents

And to one he gave five talents, to another two, and to another one, to each according to his own ability; and immediately he went on a journey.

Then he who had received the five talents went and traded with them, and made another five talents.

And likewise he who had received two gained two more also.

But he who had received one went and dug in the ground and hid his lord's money.

After a long time the lord of those servants came and settled accounts with them.

So he who had received five talents came and brought five other talents, saying, 'Lord, you delivered to me five talents; look, I have gained five more talents besides them.'

His Lord said to him, 'Well done, good and faithful servant; you were faithful over a few things, I will make you ruler over many things. Enter into the joy of your lord.'

He also who had received two talents came and said, 'Lord, you delivered to me two talents; look, I have gained two more talents beside them.

His lord said to him, 'Well done, good and faithful servant; you have been faithful over a few things, I will make you ruler over many things. Enter into the joy of your Lord.

Then he who had received the one talent came and said, 'Lord, I knew you to be a hard man, reaping where you have not sown, and gathering where you have not scattered seed.

'And I was afraid, and went and hid your talent in the ground. Look, there you have what is yours.'

But his lord answered and said to him, 'You wicked and lazy servant, you knew that I reap where I have not sown, and gather where I have not scattered seed.

'So you ought to have deposited my money with the bankers, and in my coming I would have received back my own with interest.'

'Therefore take the talent from him, and give it to him who has ten talents.'

'For to everyone who has, more will be given, and he will have abundance; but from him who does not have, even what he has will be taken away.'

Matthew 25:15-29

When I was growing up, my friend and I used to debate on who was the best group, the Miracles or the Temptations. I conceded that even though the Temptations were more versatile, they could not sing without Smokey Robinson, their songwriter. In Part Three of this book, you will read about the greatness of Paul Robeson who was multitalented and was given many talents and leveraged them into more talents. Paul Robeson reminds me of my pastor Jeremiah Wright, Jr. who is also multitalented. He can preach the sermon, teach the sermon, sing the sermon, musically play the sermon, and translate the sermon into more than five different languages!

In one of my earlier books, *Motivating and Preparing Black Youth for Success*, I said that developing your talent is a greater motivator than money. The Lord has given all of us talents, and it hurts to know that some people will go their entire lives without ever having identified them. Like the last servant in the parable, they bury their talents and end up working jobs rather than leveraging them into careers and businesses. I believe that when you begin to identify, develop, and use your talents, you'll love what you do so much you'd be willing to do it for free—but because you do it so well, you get paid!

New Wineskins

No one puts a piece of unshrunk cloth on an old garment; for the patch pulls away from the garment, and the tear is made worse.

Nor do they put new wine into old wineskins, or else the wine skins break, the wine is spilled, and the wineskins are ruined. But they put new wine into new wineskins, and both are preserved.

Matthew 9:16-17

There are many individuals and institutions that are guilty of running their lives and their operations by pouring new wine into old wineskins. Why? Because as the old saying goes, that's the way they've always done it. If you keep doing what you're doing, you will keep getting what you're getting. If you are continually having problems in your relationships, it is time to consider putting new wine into new wineskins. If you are consistently having financial problems, it is time to consider a new financial strategy.

Today's Black leaders should not operate with the same wine that was used by Martin Delany, Frederick Douglass, Booker T. Washington, and W.E.B. DuBois. Marches, sit-ins, and boycotts may not capture today's youth. Our ancestors would be extremely disappointed if they reviewed the current voter's registration and turnout percentages of African American youth. What type of wine will motivate our youth? What type of wine will help them to no longer associate being smart with acting White? What type of wine will be necessary for African Americans to spend more than 3 percent of their $500 billion with other African American businesses?

The Speck vs. The Plank

And why do you look at the speck in your brother's eye, but do not perceive the plank in your own eye?

Or how can you say to your brother, 'Brother, let me remove the speck that is in your eye,' when you yourself do not see the plank that is in your own eye? Hypocrite! First remove the plank from your own eye, and then you will see clearly to remove the speck that is in your brother's eye.

Luke 6:41-42

Why does the Black community react with rage when a white person commits a hate crime against an African American and almost silent when African Americans do it to each other? How is it that African American men can articulate the problems of racism yet don't see how denying African American women access to the pulpit contradicts the value of inclusion? Date rape and marital rape are running rampant. How can a pastor, who has committed adultery numerous times with his parishioners, ostracize homosexuals from the church?

When your hand points at someone, have you ever noticed that the majority of the fingers point back at you?

Michael Jackson reminds us that we all need to look in the mirror before we begin to look out the window. I know that it is easier to point fingers at others than to do the necessary inner work that's required to make changes. Unfortunately, many people make an attempt to improve their self-esteem by destroying others.

My House on the Rock

He is like a man building a house, who dug deep and laid the foundation on the rock. And when the flood arose, the stream beat vehemently against that house, and could not shake it, for it was founded on the rock.

Luke 6:48

Did you notice that the stream vehemently beat against the house? Bad things happen to good people. Ask Job and Joseph. Ask African American women who have been sexually faithful to their husbands and now are dying of AIDS. This makes me think of Jesus' words in John 16:33: "In the world you will have tribulation; but be of good cheer, I have overcome the world." We have been given the formula that can reduce our divorce rate, which is a staggering 66 percent.

This story teaches that if we dig deep, if we pray and read scripture, our house on the rock will withstand the floods. Unless the house is on the rock, everything else will be sinking sand. It is foolish to be more concerned about the outside of the house than its foundation. Some of us do a better job with our lawns than sweeping, mopping, and vacuuming the floor inside. Some of us bought a house, but never built a home.

A Harvest

'The harvest truly is plentiful, but the laborers are few.

Therefore pray the Lord of the harvest to send our laborers into His harvest.'

Matthew 9:37-38

Have you noticed in your organization the same few people do the majority of the work? Ever heard of the 10 percent theory that 10 percent of the people do 90 percent of the work? Have you ever wondered why? Is it because the leaders lack a vision or organizational skills? Is it because of the peculiarities of your institution?

It continues to amaze me how African American men respond to the call for mentoring, rites of passage, and crime watch groups in large numbers, but as soon as the real work begins, the numbers dramatically decline. Could it be that we lack accountability? Is it because there are no consequences? Are the 10 percent power hungry and obsessed with the desire to be needed by the 90 percent?

The Prodigal Son

A certain man had two sons.
'Father, give me the portion of goods that falls to me.' So he divided to them his livelihood.

And not many days after, the younger son gathered all together, journeyed to a far country, and there wasted his possessions with prodigal living.

But when he had spent all, there rose a severe famine in that land, and he began to be in want.

Then he went and joined himself to a citizen of that county, and he sent him into his fields to feed swine.

And he would gladly have filled his stomach with the pods that the swine ate, and no one gave him anything.

But when he came to himself, he said, 'How many of my father's hired servants have bread enough and to spare, and I perish with hunger!'

'I will arise and go to my father, and will say to him, 'Father, I have sinned against heaven and before you, and I am no longer worthy to be called your son. Make me like one of your hired servants.'

And he rose and came to his father. But when he was still a great way off, his father saw him and had compassion, and ran and fell on his neck and kissed him.

And the son said to him, 'Father, I have sinned against heaven and in your sight, and am no longer worthy to be called your son.'

But the father said to his servants, 'Bring out the best robe and put it on him, and put a ring on his hand and sandals on his feet.

'And bring the fatted calf here and kill it, and let us eat and be merry, for this my son was dead and is alive again; he was lost and is found.' And they began to be merry.

Now his older son was in the field. And as he came and drew near to the house, he heard music and dancing.

So he called one of the servants and asked what these things meant.

And he said to him, 'Your brother has come, and because he has received him safe and sound, your father has killed the fatted calf.'

But he was angry and would not go in. Therefore his father came out and pleaded with him.

So he answered and said to his father, 'Lo, these many years I have been serving you; I never transgressed your commandment at any time; and yet you never gave me a young goat, that I might make merry with my friends.'

'But as soon as this son of yours came, who has devoured your livelihood with harlots, you killed the fatted calf for him.'

And he said to him, 'Son, you are always with me, and all that I have is yours.'

'It was right that we should make merry and be glad, for your brother was dead and is alive again, and was lost and is found.'

Luke 15:11-32

To be africentric is to have an African frame of reference. We see the world through African eyes. There are at least four different frames of reference in this story: the biological father, the prodigal son, the resentful brother, and Jesus. Depending upon your own frame of reference you will identify with one character more than another.

Imagine yourself as the faithful brother who stayed with the father, worked hard and was very diligent and trustworthy with his financial resources. How would you feel if your irresponsible sibling returned home to a celebration you have never received? If we live in a world where there is no mercy and grace but only justice, it is easy to understand the brother's point of view. Imagine being the prodigal son and the humbling experience of returning home with nothing to a father who loves you unconditionally and has placed your sins as far as the east is from the west, to be remembered no more. The biological father thought like Jesus and loved his child more than the money he squandered.

Other parables that the greatest Storyteller shared with his disciples and followers were The Mustard Seed, The Ungrateful Debtor, The Shepherd and His Sheep, The Child and the Kingdom, The Good Samaritan, The Vine and the Fruit, The Narrow Gate, The Rich Man in Heaven, The Rich Man in Hell, The Poor Widow, The Grateful Samaritan, and The Tax Collector. Jesus clearly understood the power of a story. People may not remember a speech or a sermon, statistics, trends, analysis, and summary, but hours, days, weeks, months, and sometimes years later the story is preserved.

PART 2

SANKOFA

History is the clock
by which a people measure their
greatness.

One of the Seven Wonders of the World

A long time ago, almost five thousand years ago, approximately 2600 B.C., more than a hundred thousand men were going to make history. They were going to show the world their genius. They had mastered the laws of math and science. Can you imagine understanding algebra, geometry, and trigonometry five thousand years ago? Their desire was to build a perfectly balanced building that was perfectly right angled and equal to the latitude at the equator. The building is almost 48 stories tall and 755 feet wide. It consists of more than two million stones, each weighing three tons.

Africans wanted to build a building that would transcend time so that no other group would say that African people had not built anything of value. They realized that if they would build an edifice hundreds of years before other groups developed their civilizations there would be no doubt who built one of the Seven Wonders of the World.

In 1978 the Japanese tried to recreate its construction, but not even 20th century technology could build it. How could Africans know way back then that if they divided the parameter, which is 3,023 feet by twice its height of 48 stories, that the yield would be 3.1428, which is a working approximation of Pi, a figure that is used by engineers today? How did African people 5,000 years ago bring 100,000 people together for 60 years to build this tremendous structure, when we can't bring 100 people together for six years to build anything?

Africans built 72 pyramids in Egypt alone. Others are found in Ethiopia and Mexico. The pyramids are a shining example of our greatness.

The Door of No Return

I can't see. It's been dark for months. There is a person lying next to me. I can't see him but, I do feel him when he urinates or defecates next to me. The stench in the dungeon is beyond words. I wanted to die weeks ago, but the spirit within me continues to persevere.

There are three little peepholes on the other side of the dungeon. I wish I was closer to those holes. One hole is for water, one for air, and the other is for food, very little of which trickles over to me. I am consumed by thoughts of my wife and our three children. I pray to God that their experience is not like mine. Periodically, pale men with long stringy hair come into the dungeon with guns to pull out those who have died.

I hear commotion outside. It sounds like it is from the ocean. Suddenly the door of the dungeon is opened. It is hard for me to see because the rays of the sun are so bright and my eyes have become filled with death. As I begin to adjust to the rays of the sun there is a big wooden ship with hundreds of other pale white men. They are poking us out of the dungeon with a long stick. We are going through the door of no return. To my left and facing east is my homeland. Africa is the home of my parents and their parents and their ancestors. It is the mother of civilization and it has given me life. To my right and to the west is the ship filled with people that I do not know, going to a place where I have never been. They have not asked me if I want to go. They didn't ask me how I felt in the dungeon.

These pale men are smart, they have chains around our wrists and chains around our ankles and we are chained to each other. If I had the opportunity to run through this door of no return I would head east. East represents life, culture, civilization, family. West represents death and the unknown. Will I ever see my family again? Will I see Africa again? I wish this was a bad dream. In the past when I had bad dreams I could always wake myself up and they would end. I would forget my bad dreams. I wish I could deaden my mind, go through the door of no return, sleep, and forget about what happened. I wonder what happens to a people who forget? I wonder what happens to people who get amnesia about the door of no return? What happens to people who never want to return back to Ghana, but rather spend their vacations in London or Paris?

Never Forget

You are the offspring of the ancestors who would not die. Some people say one million Africans died in the slave trade. Others say that it was equivalent to the six million Jews that died in Germany. Others have increased the figures to 20 million. Some say it's 40 to 60 million. Others feel that it was as high as 100 million if you include Africans who resisted being caught on African soil, those who died in the dungeons, on the slave ships, and on the plantations.

We are the offspring of the people who survived. Had our ancestors died in the dungeon, jumped overboard on the ship, or killed themselves on the plantation you would not be reading this story. There is something special about you. You have endured the world's greatest oppression and still you smile, laugh, and make beautiful music. You built the first civilization and you made America the richest country in the world. Neither could have happened without you. There is something special about you and everybody seems to know it but you. You are the fastest in the hundred meters and the marathon. You knock someone's brain out in the boxing ring and you can put his brain back together in the emergency room.

You must never forget to tell your story to your children. If you miss telling one generation about the pyramids, the door of no return, and all you've endured, your children will become cynical. They will talk back to you. They will associate being smart with acting White. They will tell teachers, "I don't want to learn any of that Black stuff."

Nat Turner

The hole that I am in reminds me of what the ancestors said about the dungeons. I am in South Hampton, Virginia. I've been in this hole for almost 60 days. On July 4, 1831, I planned the greatest insurrection in American history. That is what July 4 means to us. Freedom, independence, the pursuit of liberty, and justice for all. We were going to make it a reality. Our original desire was to actually start the insurrection on this day, but I knew my men were not ready. We knew about the success and failure of Gabriel Prosser in Virginia and Denmark Vesey in South Carolina. Some Negroes had learned to hate themselves from Willie Lynch and had more loyalty for their oppressors than each other. No one was going to be in my insurrection whom I could not trust.

My wife, Cherry helped develop the insurrection strategy. We waited until the night of August 22 before we killed our owner and every white person—man, woman, and child—who lived in the house. Ten days later, more than 60 whites had been killed. Whites in the surrounding area would never sleep comfortably again. They knew that the African spirit for freedom could not be squelched. They knew it was only a matter of time before there would be freedom for everyone.

I believe in my Lord and Savior Jesus Christ. They can't take my life; I can lay it down. I am not afraid of death. I could have snuck out of Virginia and into Pennsylvania and freedom, but how could I leave Cherry and my children? What kind of man would I be in Pennsylvania while my wife, was being severely tortured and unaware of my whereabouts? I don't know how long I can stay in this cave. I've dug a tunnel from the cave to my previous owner's house. They would never think I was living up under the house.

I pray that no Negro tells them where I am staying. I am only 31 years of age, and I know I am going to die soon. My prayer is that my offspring never forget that there is a price for freedom, and you must be willing to pay for it.

Harriet Tubman

Harriet said freedom is only for those bold enough to take it. At the young age of seven she made her first attempt for freedom. She was called the Moses of her people. She became very frustrated one time when she was attempting to break away and a man became tired and hungry and wanted to return. Tubman pointed a gun at him and said "move or die." She was very concerned that if they went back, they would be made to reveal the locations of the various houses that made up the Underground Railroad. She refused to let that happen.

But to me the greatest legacy of Harriet Tubman, beyond the 300 people she led out of slavery and brought to freedom, is the fact that she risked her life to return to the South 19 times. Can you imagine the risk that was involved? She was already free. She could have remained in Pennsylvania, New York, or Canada. Each subsequent return to the South increased the bounty on her life. Would you have gone back 19 times? Would you have gone back once? Harriet realized at a very early age that none of us are free until all of us are free.

Queen Nzingha

She was Queen and General of Angola. She was a military genius. Her favorite strategies were surprise attacks and infiltrating enemy ranks. The Portuguese were trying to control Angola. They were effectively using the theory of divide and conquer and were pitting Africans against Africans. Queen Nzingha took advantage of this and literally had more of her soldiers in their ranks than they had. She successfully warded off the attacks of the Portuguese for more than 40 years.

Not only was she a great military genius, she was an intense negotiator. The Governor of Portugal called for negotiations and a treaty to be established between the Portuguese and the Angolans. In the meeting room the Governor had his executive cabinet and military officers all around him and he was comfortably sitting in a chair. When the Queen entered with her men, the executive council and military officers did not stand to greet her. The Governor smirked. He designed the room so that the only chair in the room would be his. Queen Nzingha was always prepared, battle field or negotiations. She knew that the Governor was arrogant, racist, and discourteous. Therefore, she brought her own accommodations. Her men rolled out the royal carpet for her. Her military officers took turns kneeling, palms to the ground, and were honored to have her sit on their back as she negotiated for the liberation of her people. The Governor then realized he was in for the fight of his life and that Queen Nzingha was going to represent her people with dignity.

Yaa Asantewaa

The Golden Stool

In Ghana, the Golden Stool represents the soul of the nation. No one had ever sat on the Golden Stool. Tradition had led Africans to believe that the Golden Stool was from God. The Ashanti King, Osei TuTu, had great respect for tradition and custom. The Ghanians had been resisting colonialist efforts from the British for more than a hundred years between 1820-1920. The British Governor demanded to sit on the Golden Stool. This irritated the Ghanian people. Led by Queen Yaa Asantewaa, the Ashanti men were led to fight harder, even though they did not have the sophisticated weaponry of the British. Unfortunately the British won the war, but to this day, the Golden Stool remains a sacred symbol for inspiring African people to withstand vicious attacks from the oppressors, and was never sat on by the British.

Unsung Heroes

Slavery ended five years ago. They promised freedom. But freedom to do what? Freedom to go where? How can I be free with no land, capital, and equipment? The only thing that changed for me since the end of the Civil War is that I am no longer a slave but a sharecropper. There never seems to be a harvest large enough to alleviate the debt. Every year Mr. Owens, the landowner, shows us more expenses than our revenue.

My wife is the most beautiful woman in the county. What people don't know is that she is prettier on the inside. We have four children, two which came from Sarah and the other two are the offspring of Sarah and Mr. Owens. I have nightmares as I think about killing Mr. Owens. I hate him. He has violated my manhood and takes advantage of my wife. He has always told me "you can have your life or your dignity, but you cannot have both."

Sarah comforts me every night as she pleads with me to choose my life. Can you imagine what it is like for me to sit on my front porch, while Mr. Owens walks right by and goes into my bedroom to do his business on my wife? I have killed him a million times in my mind. It is becoming harder to look into the eyes of my wife. Years ago I stopped looking into the eyes of my children. The pain was too great and they didn't understand. I've begun to reach a point where I would rather die with dignity than to live like this.

Tonight Mr. Owens walked into my house for the last time. Five minutes later I walked in behind him. He was in my bed, nude and on top of my wife. I was filled with rage. I grabbed him and began to choke him. Sarah pleaded to let him go. She knew that if I killed him white men from around the entire county would lynch me and my family. Something happened to me that night. My manhood was uncompromising. My love for freedom had now exceeded death. Twenty years of rage was expressed in twenty seconds as I choked the life out of Mr. Owens. As he dropped to the floor, I told Sarah to get up, get the children ready, take whatever they could take within minutes, and we left Monroe County. We've never been seen since.

The Unveiling of the Flag

On August 2, 1920, more than 20,000 African Americans gathered at Madison Square Garden in New York, which, at the time, was the largest indoor auditorium in the country. The UNIA (Universal Negro Improvement Association) convened this meeting to develop a 54-statement Bill of Rights. Their motto was "Africa for the Africans, Let Africa be Our Guiding Star." The participants of that historic meeting declared that night that the word "Negro" was going to be capitalized.

Then the leader of the UNIA movement entered onto the main stage. There was a 15-minute standing ovation for the young printer from Jamaica whose vision included Black-owned ships, stores, newspapers, banks, and churches. When the crowd finally took their seats, Marcus Garvey unveiled the liberation flag, the red the black, and the green. Red for the blood, black for the people, and green for the land. The Black nation would never be the same again. Marcus Garvey went on to organize more than a million people to promote the concept of Black nationalism.

Rule 110

Remember a long time ago, before 1954, before Brown vs. Topeka? Remember the one-room school house for Black children where there were 40 students and only two books, yet everyone learned? The older students helped the younger students, and everyone tried to encourage each other to be the best. Black teachers daily reminded African American students they had to be twice as good in order to make it in this country. We were not allowed to turn in ragged sheets of paper. They were rejected and we had to redo them. In order to receive an "A," you had to have a score greater than 100. It was called Rule 110. Students were always trying to get extra credit because that was the only way to receive an "A."

We were not allowed to wear caps in the building, nor were we allowed to curse and talk back to our teachers. Before 1954, schools did not believe in social promotion. If a child could not read past fourth grade, his or her butt did not go past fourth grade. Today many teachers have lowered the standards for African American youth, and some African American students have accepted the myth of inferiority. They plead with teachers to give them a grade because they are Black, fatherless, and low-income. Some of today's children associate smart with being White. Remember a long time ago when being smart meant being Black meant being the best? What happened? Did it happen in 1954? Did we get what we wanted and lost what we had? How many of today's teachers pull African American children to the side and remind them that they have to be twice as good as Whites to make it in America?

The next four stories are not as positive as the preceding stories. They illustrate the tragedy of a people who have bought into self-hatred. The stories are humorous and tragic. When Moses chose one of each tribe to scout and spy on the promised land, Caleb and Joshua came back with a positive report. Caleb said that they were well able to overcome them. That is the kind of spirit we need today. We need more people to have a Caleb spirit, but unfortunately most of us follow the majority report. The other ten reported back to Moses that the Canaanites were giants—and they saw themselves as grasshoppers. The following four stories are illustration of a people who act like grasshoppers.

What Is Wrong With Us?

A couple needed plumbing in their house. An African American business bidded $800. The couple said that there was no way that they were going to pay a Black man that kind of money to do the work and asked him to leave. The next day they called a White general contractor out to bid on the exact same job and they said it would cost $1,000. The couple said yes and accepted their offer. Several days later the Black contractor knocked on the door and the couple said, "We told you that we did not want you to do the work," and they asked him to leave. But before they could close the door the Black contractor told them, "I came out here several days ago and bidded $800 as a favor to you and you said no. I work for that White contractor who bidded $1,000, and now I am here to do their work."

My Skin

(Inspired by Bob Law)

Branch Rickey, the former general manager of the Brooklyn Dodgers who spearheaded the move of Jackie Robinson into the major leagues, describes an incident with another one of his Black ballplayers. At that time he was in the minor leagues and was traveling with the team from city to city. It was time to check into the hotel. The White hotel manager checked in all of the White ballplayers but told Branch Rickey that his Black ballplayer would not be allowed in the hotel. Branch Rickey argued with the hotel manager to no avail and checked him into a colored hotel.

Later that evening, Branch Rickey checked in to see how he was doing. When he opened the door, he saw his star on the floor, crying and rubbing his skin with a washcloth. He hollered at Branch Rickey and said, "It's my skin. It's my skin. I would be able to stay at the white hotel if it was not for my skin." He continued his crying and wiping. "It's my skin. It's my skin." Branch Rickey said, "No son, the problem is not your skin. The problem is with us."

A Safety Net

Yesterday afternoon after school, a White teenager named Joey, who didn't have anything else to do after school, threw a rock through a cleaners' window. Later that evening, the three White men who owned the business visited Joey and said that they had reports that he was the one who threw the rock. They then explained to Joey that the window would cost $275.00. They asked Joey about his activities after school. When Joey said he had nothing to do, they told Joey that he was incorrect because starting tomorrow he would have a part-time job working in their cleaners. They then told Joey that the first monies that he earned would be used to repay them for the window. Then they told Joey, because they were getting older and none had sons, they were interested in trying to identify someone to take over the business. They promised Joey that if he worked hard and followed directions, they would reserve 25 percent of his check and invest it in a mutual fund, and this money could be used as a scholarship for college. Joey would receive mentoring on a regular basis.

That same day across town a Black male teenager committed the same violation. He threw a rock through a store window, but unfortunately, the business was not owned by African Americans. It was owned by Whites,

Jews, Arabs, or Asians. For some reason he did not receive a visit from the owner offering a part-time job, a scholarship, mutual funds, mentorship, and entrepreneurial classes. He was shot in the back and is now facing five years in both the juvenile system and the adult prison.

The Dollar Bill Story

A dollar bill and a twenty-dollar bill had been friends from the very beginning. They enjoyed being together. They had been produced in the same printing press within days of each other. When they first started, they were inseparable. They had gone overseas together and went on cruises and safaris. They stayed at the finest hotels and loved going to Disney World, Disney Land, and Great America. They enjoyed being at some of the finest restaurants in the world. They loved going to concerts where Maxwell and Tony Braxton performed.

Unfortunately one day they got separated and the dollar bill landed in church. For some reason, in this institution, the dollar bill is the most popular bill in the congregation. Parishioners seemed obsessed with the dollar bill, never wanting it to leave. They started putting the dollar bill in the offering as teenagers. When they became adults and elders, they were still putting in a dollar bill.

The dollar bill became very lonely. He missed traveling and going to nice hotels, restaurants, concerts, and cruises. He wondered where his friend, the twenty-dollar bill, might be at this time. The dollar bill used to go through the giving basket looking for his five, ten, and twenty-dollar friends. Unfortunately all he ever saw were other dollar bills that looked like him. Finally one day a twenty-dollar bill was in the basket and the dollar bill found him. He was so exited. He said, "Where have you been?" The twenty-dollar bill said, "Where have *you* been? We have been looking all over for you." The dollar bill said, "Remember that day we got separated? Well, I have been stuck in this church for the last twenty years. They won't let me out; they love me. They use me for every offering." The dollar bill then asked the twenty dollar bill, "Where have *you* been?" The twenty-dollar bill smiled and said, "I'm still going to our favorite places, but I've also been to exotic islands, consuming tropical drinks, laying up on the beach, and thinking about you."

PART 3

POWER

The following stories are about individuals and their will to survive. win, and succeed. I can think of no better illustration of power than to share with you some of the most fantastic stories about individuals whose spirit would not allow them to fail.

Frederick Douglass

What comes to your mind when you think about Frederick Douglass? The editor of the North Star Newspaper? The famous Black leader who had access to Abraham Lincoln's office? Do you think about the great writer and orator? One of his most famous speeches was how Africans feel about July 4 and that hypocrisy that still exists in America.

When I think of Frederick Douglass I don't think of the man, I think of the nine-year-old little boy who would sneak out the back door with his books almost every night. Using candlelight or on good evenings moonlight, he would teach himself to read. Douglass loved the written word and liked being able to read the thoughts of others. He loved traveling around the world through books. Books opened up his horizons, expanded his world view.

Unfortunately, almost every night that Douglass snuck out the back door, his owner caught him and would strip him and beat him. They beat him badly. Even as an adult you could still see some of the scars on his back. Yet the very next day, Douglass was sneaking out the backdoor again with his candle and his books. He must have decided that knowing how to read and being educated was important and threatening to the oppressors. Douglass used the beatings to inspire him to read more.

Paul Robeson

Very few people have been blessed with as many talents as Paul Robeson. He was a brilliant scholar. One year in high school he received six "A's" and one "B" and his father was not pleased about the "B." Paul corrected that mistake and never received another "B" again. He went on to become the valedictorian of his college class at Rutgers University. He was a brilliant singer. His voice was strong and the world demanded to hear him and he sang to sold out audiences. He loved the stage and received numerous awards for his stellar performance in *Othello*. He also loved the silver screen and received awards for his performance in *Emperor Jones.*

Robeson spoke 20 languages, graduated from Columbia Law School, and became a lawyer. While working at a white law firm, a white stenographer told Paul Robeson "I don't take dictation from a nigger." Paul then decided that he was not going to be treated like a nigger and left the law firm to pursue his other talents.

To me the greatest story about Paul Robeson and his indomitable spirit was not about his experiences on the stage, screen, the law office, in the classroom, or when the Senate grilled him in hearings about his relationships with communists. To me the greatest story is about Paul Robeson, the athlete. He lettered in four sports—football, basketball, baseball, and track. The Rutgers coach solicited Paul for football because he desperately wanted to beat his arch rival Princeton. But Paul's teammates had mutinied against the coach and said that they would not play with a Black man. The coach forced them to go back out on the field. His teammates proceeded in practice to break his nose and dislocate his shoulder. On one particular play, Robeson had tackled the fullback. His teammates spiked his hands and they were bleeding profusely. On the very next play that same running back was given the ball. Paul did more than tackle him, he picked him up over his head and held him in front of his team mates who were in awe of his strength and tenacity. From that day, Paul was accepted by his teammates and made captain of the team.

Nelson Mandela

I used to be a boxer, but now I am a political prisoner. I am a husband and father, but they only allow Winnie to see me every six months. They harass her every time she comes, and I am only allowed to write her once every six months. They read most of my letters. I used to be a lawyer, but now I am a political prisoner. My "crime" is that I am a freedom fighter.

I am a member of the African National Congress (ANC). Our crime is that we were meeting together to discuss our freedom. Geronimo Pratt was a political prisoner who stayed in jail for the same number of years I did—27 years. Mumia Abu-Jamal remains a political prisoner.

My cell is about one foot longer than my height, and it is not fit for an animal. I have had almost 27 years of porridge. This is designed to destroy you mentally and physically. Some of our members were on the verge of breaking down. Had it not been for our unity, we would not have been able to keep each other from cracking.

What happens to a dream deferred? Does it dry up like a raisin in the sun? asked Langston Hughes. How does someone remain in jail for 27 years and go from prisoner to President? How does someone who did not commit a crime remain in prison for 27 years? Yet Mandela has no bitterness in his heart but only a love for his people.

I will never forget when former South African President Deklerk quickly decided that he was going to release Nelson Mandela to try to calm the mood of angry Africans who were furious over the incarceration of their leader. Deklerk told Mandela that he was going to release him the very next day. Mandela said, "I will determine when I leave." After 27 years in jail Nelson Mandela said, "That was too soon." He wanted to talk to his fellow inmates. He wanted to discuss and negotiate their release. He wanted his family to be present. He wanted his international friends to be present at his release. He wanted to thank those guards who, over the years, began to act human and saw him as a human being. He wanted the ANC to be involved in the coordination of his first speech in front of his people, and he wanted it to be planned properly without being rushed.

Nelson Mandela is a man of integrity. After his release he visited the United States and was interviewed on *Nightline* by Ted Koppel. Koppel wanted Nelson Mandela to denounce Gadhafi. Koppel has a great admiration for Nelson Mandela and told him, "You don't understand. America does not like Gadhafi. It is not in your political interest to stick to your position." Nelson Mandela looked Koppel dead in the eye and said, "You don't understand, Ted. I am not a politician. My beliefs do not change based on my location or who is in my company. I am an African, and Gadhafi is my friend and supported me when I was incarcerated."

Jesse Owens

It was 1936. He was the son of a sharecropper who suffered from bronchitis and pneumonia. He attended Ohio State University on a full track scholarship and became their first Black captain. He was now competing in front of 100,000 Germans, including Adolph Hitler. It had been a great Olympics for Jesse Owens, but it was painful for Adolph Hitler. As he had stood on the winner's circle to receive four gold medals—in the 100 meters, 200 meters, 400-meter relay, and the long jump—Owens was snubbed by Adolph Hitler, who did not even watch the ceremony. When Jesse Owens returned home to the United States, he was also snubbed by the President.

Ironically, the person who befriended him the most, to the disdain of Adolph Hitler, was Luz Long, the best long jumper in the world at that time. Adolph Hitler and the Germans were very confident that Jesse Owens would never receive his fourth gold medal. In the preliminaries of the long jump, Luz Long, on his very first jump, easily qualified at the distance of 24 feet. Unfortunately, Jesse Owens failed on his first attempt to make the qualifying mark. Luz Long went over to Jesse, put his arm around his shoulder, and said, "What's wrong with you is that you are afraid you will foul again. Why don't you alter your take off? That way it is impossible to foul." Jesse qualified with an unofficial world record.

The following day in the finals, these two great athletes of two different races realized that they were part of the human race and provided the greatest competition in the 1936 Olympics. Luz jumped first, Jesse jumped further. Luz jumped further. Jesse then jumped a little further. The crowd was on their feet with every jump. On Luz's third jump he broke the world record and the German crowd was ecstatic. Adolph Hitler continued to believe in a master race theory.

Then it was Jesse Owens' final jump. He was nervous. He had worked so hard for gold medals. He looked over at his mentor Charles Rile who nodded a word of encouragement. He looked over at his teammates, and they too were nodding words of encouragement. Before Jesse Owens made his final jump, he looked at his new friend. You could tell in his eyes Luz was cheering him on to "go a little further." Jesse knew when he ran down the runway that this would be the new world record. He seemed to have stayed in the air forever. Jesse had broken the world record. They hugged each other and Hitler left the stadium.

Ben Carson

Months earlier Dr. Ben Carson had just separated the brains of Siamese twins from Germany. He was now scrubbing for what was going to be a 28-hour surgery to separate another set of twins whose brains remained lodged together.

He reflected on his own life. He thought about his wife Candy and his children. He thought about how difficult it had been growing up in Detroit. He and his brother were very poor and without a father. He had failed fourth grade. His mother was furious and made him turn off the television and read a book once a week. She then made him write about what he read. Books ultimately became his love and saving grace.

The man they now call Gentle Ben had a terrible temper back then. Once, someone made a derogatory comment about his mother and he stabbed him. The Lord heard his cry as he screamed, "Take away my temper. I'll give my mind, my brains, my hands to You." Now when he scrubs his hands, he looks to the sky and says, "Hallelujah!" The hands that were once used to almost kill someone are now being used to save lives.

Wilma Rudolph

"Runners, take your mark!" The gun is in the air. Wilma is in the starting block for the 100 meters in Rome, Italy, 1960. The starter seems to be holding them in the blocks forever. Her entire life races in front of her.

Born in 1940 with polio in Clarksville, Tennessee, they said she would never walk. At age four, she had double pneumonia and scarlet fever. A metal brace was placed on her left leg and was not taken off until she was 12 years of age. As the starter holds them in the blocks, she thinks about the 200 meters to be run later in the day and the 400-meter relay later in the week. Her goal was to be the first Black woman to win three gold medals. She is ready to run and the starter won't shoot the gun.

She thinks about her 21 siblings and how demanding 22 children were on her mother and father. Her track coach from Tennessee State is there to cheer her on and she looks up just for a moment and makes eye contact. The starter still does not shoot the gun. It has become a test of will and concentration. A race that will only take ten seconds is now being held in the starting blocks for almost ten minutes. She keeps hearing this tape in the back of her mind, "She'll never walk again, she'll never walk again, she'll never walk again." Boom! The gun shoots.

Wilma is the first out of the blocks. She can see the tape at the finish line. It is going to be a close race. She leans. She wins.

Later she would tell young people that doctors do not have the final say over your life, and that ultimately, it is between you and the Lord.

Martin and Malcolm

How long? Not long. Martin and Malcolm knew they didn't have much time. In Benjamin Mays' famous poem he illuminates how time is fleeting: "Sixty seconds in a minute, a lifetime depends on it." In the average lifespan of 70 years, people will spend 23 years sleeping, 16 years working, 8 years watching television, 6 years eating, 6 years commuting, $4^{1}/_{2}$ years for leisure, 4 years ill, 2 years dressing, and 6 months involved in religion.

Martin and Malcolm knew they wouldn't have 70 years. They were hoping they could get more than 60 seconds in a minute. Malcolm spent from 1925 to 1938 being a good student. From 1938 to 1946, he was separated from his family and became a hustler. He was incarcerated from 1946 to 1952 and became Malcolm X. He only had 13 years from 1952 to 1965 to share his brilliance with his people.

How long? Not long. Sixty seconds in a minute. Martin Luther King knew he didn't have much time. He graduated from Booker T. Washington High School at 15, Morehouse College at 19, Crozier with a master degree at 22, Boston University with a doctorate at 26, and died at 39. Thirteen years to try to save the world. It is not *how* long you live, but *what* you do while you are alive. You can live 70 years of age and accomplish very little. Are you going to spend your years merely sleeping, watching television, and eating? Martin and Malcolm did their best with 39 years. Our Lord and Savior Jesus Christ only had 33 years.

Muhammad Ali

This is not going to be easy. It is Round 2 in the Heavyweight Championship of the world, and Ken Norton has just broken Muhammad Ali's jaw. Norton does not know it, but the Ali camp is very worried. Muhammad sits in his corner at the end of the round. He wonders how he is going to fight 13 rounds with a broken jaw. He has claimed the Heavyweight title three times, never done before Ali.

He thinks of all of the years he lost in his prime because he chose not to fight the White man's war in Vietnam. "Move like a butterfly, sting like a bee" became Muhammad's motto. In more than 100 victories, the two he remembers most were with his arch rival and good friend Joe Frazier. "What's my name?" he used to holler at boxers and reporters.

This would be Muhammad's greatest test. No one would know about his jaw except his corner until the end of the fight. He knows that if he takes another blow to his jaw there will be permanent damage. He wonders if he can finish, much less win the fight, but there is something special about Ali. During the last 13 rounds, he found a source of power that he didn't have in the first two rounds. He wins the fight. He is not hollering "What's My Name?" or "I float like a butterfly and sting like a bee." Instead he is pleading "Get me a doctor as soon as you can."

Reginald Lewis

It is unfortunate that many people don't understand money management. Many place commas and decimal points in wrong places. Once they surpass the thousands, many people confuse millions, billions, and trillions. But there was one man who knew exactly where the decimal points and commas should be placed.

Reginald Lewis grew up in a working class family. He graduated from Virginia State University and Harvard Law School. He mastered the principle of OPM (Other People's Money). He leveraged assets to buy one company at $22 million. He subsequently sold this for $90 million. He then leveraged this to buy Beatrice Foods for $985 million. He had to overcome numerous obstacles of racism. He was a tireless worker and died at 50 years of age. At his funeral, Bill Cosby eulogized, "We all are dealt a hand, and Reggie played the hell out of his hand."

Jackie Joyner Kersee

It is June 1998 in New York City. It will be her last competition in the Heptathalon. Reporters ask, "What was your greatest moment?" It is hard for Jackie to answer. She can barely breathe. She has had a constant bout with asthma. Many times she has had to wear a handkerchief over her face to filter the air.

Yet she ponders the question. Was it those championships in track and basketball in East St. Louis, Illinois? She remembers times when she was so angry at Bobby, her husband and coach, for pushing her so hard, times when she said to herself, "It is easy for you to say it but I've got to do it." She would then go home and make dinner for a man who rode her back for six hours. Was that the greatest moment? Or was it when she won the silver medal in 1984, the gold medals in 1988 and 1992, or the bronze medal in 1996? Was it when she broke the world record in the Heptathalon?

Jackie still cannot answer; she can barely breathe. It is her last event. She is considered the greatest female athlete in the world. The reporters think that her greatest moment would have to be today's performance. She hadn't competed in the Heptathalon in two years. It came down to the last race, the 800 meters, which she hated with disdain. "I'd much rather hurdle, run a sprint, throw the javelin or the shot, or my favorite event the long jump, but why the 800 meters?" She wins her final Heptathalon.

She surprises her crowd and says, "My greatest achievement was the 1996 Olympics. It wasn't gold, it wasn't silver, it wasn't even a Heptathalon, or a world record. I was injured and my leg was wrapped and few if anyone expected me to win a medal in the long jump. I had never been more proud to accept that bronze medal."

Michael Jordan

I love his phrase, "I'm not afraid to fail." It concerns me that at a Black high school 300 boys will try out for the basketball team and less than five will try out for the debate team or compete in the science fair. Why does someone leave the NBA as the leading scorer in the league to try baseball, a game in which he was only mediocre? "I'm not afraid to fail." Why does somebody try out for the junior varsity basketball team in high school and fail and try again the following year and succeed? "I'm not afraid to fail." Why does someone leave college at the end of his sophomore year only to return back to college with a degree?

Why does Michael spend almost as much time on the golf course as he does on the basketball court when he's only mediocre? Again Michael responds, "I'm not afraid to fail. I work hard," says Michael. "I shoot 300 jump shots almost everyday in practice. I hate to lose."

It is game four of the eastern finals and Michael is dehydrated. Miami knows they can win this game. Michael can barely walk and see the basket. The Bulls call a time-out and Scottie Pippen literally carries him off the court. Why did Michael go back out on the court? How did the Bulls win that game? He's not afraid to fail.

Les Brown

My friend had to overcome numerous obstacles. He grew up in poverty to a single mother and was placed in special education classes and was told he would never amount to anything. He wanted a television show that would be positive, uplifting, and motivational. Unfortunately, viewers still seemed to respond more to Jerry Springer and Ricki Lake and his show was canceled. He has had a serious bout with prostrate cancer and Les continues to fight.

I love his stories, especially the one in which he and his son were playing a computer game and Les was killing him. After awhile, he said he was going to bed, but his son, who has some of Les' spirit, said, "It's not over until I win." Les responded, "I am not going to let you beat me." The son said, "You won't have to." They continued to play, and Les continued to win. Finally his son won a game. He looked his father dead in the eye and said, "Now you can go to bed because remember, it's not over until I win."

Les had done many things in his life before being a television talk show host, public speaker, author, and politician. Les was a radio disc jockey. He did more than play music, he also kept the community informed and read his scathing editorials to hold people accountable. One particular editorial exposed a music promoter who was bringing in an act that was not the original group. Unbeknownst to Les, a contract was placed on his life.

Now after work, on his way home, Les would visit a local hospital and visit the sick. He would talk with them and encourage them and was well received. Late one evening as he was walking down the street a man appeared before him and said, "Are you Les Brown?" "Yes." The man said, "I have a contract on your life." Les then asked him, "Are you going to kill me?" The man said, "No. When I heard they had a contract out on your life, I took the contract because I wanted to protect you. You see, one of the people that you visited in the hospital was my mother. She has never been the same since your visit. Go in peace, my brother."

PART 4

HOPE AND JOY

The world can give you happiness,
but only God can give you joy.

The Hardest Question

The Sterlings were a beautiful family. They had four children, two boys and two girls. Karen Sterling was beautiful and an engineer, and her husband, Bill, was considered one of the best surgeons in the country.

One relaxing Saturday afternoon, Bill was enjoying a college football game on TV. The children ran into his study and said, "Daddy, Daddy, take us to the store, take us to the store." Bill said, "I'll be there in a minute. Just one more play." Finally, Karen said, "Don't worry about it, honey. I'll take the children to the store, and you can stay home and relax and enjoy your game." Bill smiled and said, "You don't mind, baby? I'll be there in a minute." Karen said, "No, it's okay."

Minutes later there was a noise, an explosion. Bill knew something was wrong and jumped out of his seat. He ran outside the house. Less than 100 yards away was his car, completely demolished. He ran to the car. Neighbors came out and called the police and the ambulance. Horror ran through Bill's mind. "Are they alive?" When he reached the car, his children were already dead. Karen was holding on to dear life. She was rushed to the hospital. They had been hit by a drunk driver named Alex.

For the past ten years, Bill has never forgiven himself or Alex, the local neighborhood drunk. The tragedy put a tremendous strain on their marriage. She told her husband on numerous occasions, "It was bad enough that we lost our four children, but that day I also lost the most caring husband a wife could have."

Suddenly the phone rings. It's the hospital. "Alex has just been hit by a car and we need you to operate." Dr. Sterling sternly says, "I can't operate on him. I hate him." The administrator says, "You took an oath as a doctor to do whatever is possible to save a life." Dr. Sterling says, "I just can't," and hangs up the phone. Karen is standing next to him. He hugs her and begins to cry, "I can't, I can't." Karen says, "I know you can't but He can." Karen drives him to the hospital to perform the hardest operation of his life.

Don't Procrastinate

My wife Rita is a spirit filled woman who is not ashamed to praise our Lord and Savior Jesus Christ wherever she goes. It was a very relaxing Sunday afternoon and we had just returned from a very excellent worship service and were enjoying each other's company over Sunday dinner. It is really easy for most people under the circumstances to stay home and enjoy the rest of the evening before another busy work week. Rita is probably the master at relaxing and resting at home.

Earlier that day, Vivian, one of our neighbors, had asked Rita if she could to come down and visit. She had a girlfriend who was ill and needed some words of encouragement. Rita agreed, dressed, and went to visit. She had a wonderful time fellowshipping, but as I told you, whenever you talk with Rita, at some point the name of Jesus Christ is going to be mentioned. The ill friend, Viola, began to ask piercing questions. "How do you know if you are saved? What do you have to do to be saved? How is it that you are so sure that you are saved, Rita?" Viola went on to describe how she had been raised in church all of her life and attended on a regular basis.

How easy it is to be in church but not in Christ. You can be saved, but not be in relationship with Him. Rita shared what the Lord had done for her. They read

Romans 10:9, "If you confess with your mouth the Lord Jesus and believe in your heart that God raised him from the dead you shall be saved." Rita encouraged Viola to read the Word and pray.

Viola and Rita had just met that day, but by the end of the conversation they were sisters in Christ. They hugged each other and tears fell freely. Before Rita left that house, she knew Viola had given her life to Christ. The next morning Rita and I drove past their house on our way to work and we saw an ambulance outside the house. Later that day, Rita called the house to find out if everything was okay. Vivian told her that Viola died that morning. What if Rita had procrastinated and chosen to visit another day? It would have been too late. That one meeting determined where Viola was going to spend eternity.

No Room in the Inn

The hotel clerk in Philadelphia had been very busy that night. There was a convention in town and literally every hotel room in the city was occupied. It was close to midnight and the clerk was beginning to do his record keeping for the evening when an elderly couple came in and asked if there was any room available in the inn. The clerk regretfully said that all of the rooms were taken. The husband looked at the wife and the wife looked at the husband and they looked very sad. They didn't know where they were going to spend the night. The clerk then offered his room. He said, "If you don't mind, you can stay in mine. It's a little office room, but it has a cot. That is all we have." The elderly man looked at the clerk and said, "You would do that for us? Thank you very much, son. You are a fine young man. Maybe someday we'll build a hotel that you will manage." The three of them chuckled.

The elderly couple went to the clerk's room and fell asleep. Several years later, the clerk received a letter from the elderly man along with a train ticket to New York City. The clerk had no idea what the elderly man wanted. He figured the elderly couple was going to provide him with a nice weekend in New York. When they met at the train station, they hugged each other. The clerk said, "You didn't have to do this for me," and the elderly man said, "I know my son." They got into his car and drove to Fifth Avenue and 34ᵗʰ Street. They got out of the car and the elderly man pointed to the building at the corner. It was a tall, elegant building. It looked like a beautiful castle. The clerk had never seen a hotel of this magnitude.

The elderly man said, "I would like for you to manage my hotel that I built for you." The young man asked, "Who are you?" The elderly man responded, "My name is William Waldorf Astor." The young clerk's name is George Boldt, and he did become the first manager of the Waldorf-Astoria Hotel.

What Do You See?

When you look at a half of glass of water, do you see a glass that is half full or half empty? When you hear that one of every ten teenage girls becomes pregnant, do you think about the one who is or the nine who are not? The media frequently reminds us that one of every three African American males is involved with the penal system. Do you think about the one who is or the two who are not?

Pastor Ozzie Smith shared with me a story told to him by his father-in-law, Benny Westbrooks. Benny gave Ozzie a sheet of plain white paper and he put a dot on the paper and asked Ozzie what did he see on the sheet. Ozzie quickly replied, "I see a small dot in the middle of the paper." Benny Westbrooks shrugged at the boy and said, "You missed the whole sheet of white paper because you were focusing on that dot." When you focus on the obstacles, you are prevented from seeing what God has already done and the possibility of what God can do.

Who Bats Last?

Little League baseball in many cities and especially in small towns has become an American pastime filled with tradition. In small towns literally the whole city comes out to support the teams.

This was the championship game of the Little League World Series. The two best teams in the entire country had converged on Pennsylvania to find out who was the best. One team was from Arizona and the other from Maryland. It was truly going to be an East-West showdown. The Arizona Ravens struck first. They batted around in the first inning. They were hitting the Maryland Tiger's curve balls and fast balls as if they were soft balls or volley balls. The Arizona team could do no wrong. Before the first inning ended they had scored nine runs. Every player on the team had scored a run.

When the Maryland team finally came off the field, the coach rallied his players around him and said in the huddle, "Who is going to score more than once this inning?" Several hands shot up. He then went on to inspire his players. "Don't worry, we bat last. They only scored nine runs. We haven't even gone to bat! Remember, it's not over until our last out. I expect each of you to score once and all of those who raised their hands to score twice. Let's see who will keep their promise."

Nothing but the Lord

It was a beautiful day for the annual company picnic. Nearly 100 employees showed up. It was an excellent opportunity for families who rarely saw each other except for this event. There were all kinds of activities—volleyball, softball, basketball, clowns, go-carts, and jump rope—and enough food to last the entire week.

Two fathers sat under a tree, watching their children and marveling at their energy level. The fathers were also reminiscing about their youth. One of the fathers said, "You see my boy over there doing somersaults in the air? He almost died at childbirth. We had to keep him in the hospital for three months. The doctors thought that he would never walk and there would always be brain imbalance." A tear softly fell down his face and he said to the other father, "It was nothing but the Lord."

He went on to tell him, "But my story doesn't end there. You see that beautiful woman over there? She is my wife. I was an alcoholic for 17 years. She should have left me a million times. Sometimes I would come home drunk late at night, knocking over things and she would do either one of two things. She would come downstairs and make me something to eat, or I would go upstairs and turn on the light and see her asleep with the Bible on her chest. I knew she had gone to sleep praying for me. It was nothing but the Lord."

Then he said, "This is my first picnic with this company. This is the first job I have been able to hold for a full year in the past two decades. I look around at the rest of you and I don't know your story, but for me, it was nothing but the Lord."

God Breaks the Glass Ceiling

(Inspired by Reverend Frederick Haynes III)

Renee was a fine looking woman. She had earned her MBA from the Harvard Business School and knew she was going to be on easy street from this point. With this degree, glass ceilings would come shattering down and husband, children, and corporate suites were on the way

The husband and children did come. He left her and their two children and has never been seen since. The corporate suite came too, but it belonged to her supervisor Ken, the Vice President. She had a nice title, Assistant to the Vice President, which meant she did most of the work and he received most of the credit. This irritated her last black nerve. She heard a rumor from the President's office that he was interested in making Renee a Vice President, but it had been vetoed by her boss who felt she needed more grooming.

This had gone on for over a decade, and Renee was feeling very frustrated. She called her best friend who just happened to be her mother. Mama always listened to her even though she didn't provide solutions. After talking with Mama, Renee felt like she could go back out and take on corporate America again. On this particular day, Mama wasn't listening as well as she usually did, and Renee was getting ticked. Throughout the conversation Mama kept singing, "You are the strength of my life. You are the source of my strength. I give you total praise." Mama's praise was stronger than her irritation, and by the end of the conversation Renee was no longer talking about her problems in corporate America. She and her Mama were crying, tears of joy as they kept singing, "You are the strength of my life. You are the source of my strength."

Renee felt ready to go to work that morning and to do battle with her boss. As she walked into the office, the secretary mentioned that the President wanted to see her immediately. She wondered what had happened. The President seldom talked with her directly, it was always through her boss. The President asked her to come in and be seated. He said, "I know that you are going to be disappointed when I tell you this, but we have transferred Ken to our East Coast office. If you don't mind, we'd like to make you the new Vice President of our national office." Renee smiled and shook hands with the President, ran down the hall to her office, got her Mama on the phone, and said, "You are the strength of my life."

✓ A Teacher's Love Story

Ms. Hudson was considered one of the best fourth grade teachers in the country. Her secret was to have high expectations for all children and to find some way to bond with them and make each feel important. Her motto was, "You can't teach a child you do not love." She believed that throughout her entire career, but this particular year she had a very challenging student named Willie Jones. He came to school poorly dressed, often with holes in his clothes. He was dirty and smelled of urine. The children laughed at Willie and made fun of him.

In past years Ms. Hudson found creative ways to prevent children from teasing each other. One of her strategies had been to hug the student being teased in hopes that this would inspire other students to do likewise. It was November, three months into the school year, and she had not hugged Willie. Every morning she prayed that the Lord would give her the love to hug Willie Jones.

This particular morning she noticed that the other students were playing and talking with each other and Willie was left alone. She came over to Willie and wrapped her arms around him and he began to cry. He told Ms. Hudson, "It's not my fault. It's not my fault. My father works two jobs to take care of ten of us. My mother died when I was three years old." Ms. Hudson continued to hug

Willie and he continued to share his pain. He said he hadn't been hugged by a woman in six years. He told Ms. Hudson please don't let him go. From that point on, the bond between Willie Jones and Ms. Hudson was inseparable. They would come to school a half hour early and talk. She walked him home after school. She picked him up on Saturday afternoon and they went on field trips. Once a month he even spent the night.

Willie Jones never forgot Ms. Hudson. When he graduated from high school, he invited her to the graduation. When Willie graduated from Morehouse College, she was there. When he graduated from Howard's Law School, Ms. Hudson was in the audience. Willie Jones is now a Judge in the Children and Family Court Division and has a picture of Ms. Hudson in his chambers.

My Daddy is the Engineer

A daddy helps his seven-year-old little boy Andre on the Amtrak train and makes sure that his seatbelt is snug and secure. The little boy takes out his coloring book and crayons. When the daddy feels that his son is comfortable he walks toward the front of the train. The car begins to fill with passengers. This Amtrak train is leaving Connecticut and is on its way to New York City. Some people on the train have briefcases and are dressed in suits and wait in great anticipation to conduct business in New York. There are family members on the train, parents and children who are excited about all the activities they will experience and the skyscrapers they will see in the "big apple."

The trip is scheduled to last 53 minutes. Halfway through the trip the train is no longer providing a smooth ride. Fear sets in and people wonder what is happening. Businessmen put down their papers and children begin to scream. The train feels like a roller coaster ride. The train is out of control. Parents who should be consoling their children are also experiencing hysteria. Several minutes later, the train returns to a normal speed and the ride becomes smoother.

One boy who was sitting across from Andre said, "Weren't you afraid? We could've died. How come you weren't afraid?" As Andre was about to answer, his father came through the front car door of the train. Andre said, "That's my daddy. He is the engineer. As long as my daddy is the engineer, there is no need to be afraid."

Sits High and Looks Low

A woman got into her car to make her usual 15-minute commute from the office to home. She exited the parking lot and a truck fell in right behind her. She turned on the radio and enjoyed the music. She never liked truckers near her, so she accelerated to leave the trucker in the wind. For some strange reason the trucker sped up. She became fearful and wondered if this was coincidental.

She decided to abandon her traditional route and detour down a side street where truckers are not allowed. She knew if a trucker went down this street her suspicions would be confirmed. She made a sudden right and the trucker did the same. She made several lefts and rights, and the trucker continued to follow with the gap narrowing. She was scared to death and wondered if the trucker was going to sexually assault her and leave her for dead.

She wondered which was closer, the gas or police station. She doubted she could make it to the police station, it was twenty blocks away, but the gas station was only four blocks. She would get to the gas station and jump out the car. The trucker got closer. She made it into the gas station, jumped out the car leaving the car door open. As she screamed into the gas station, the trucker jumped out of the truck and into the car. He pulled a man from the back seat. The woman stared in disbelief. She thought she was running from the trucker who sits high and looks low, while a thief was in the back seat of her car. Our God also sits high and looks low. We often run from God while Satan is in our back seat.

Checkmate

In a very famous art gallery in London hangs a famous portrait titled "Checkmate." It's a picture of Nephistopheles and Dr. Faust. The picture illustrates a chess board. On one side of the chess board is the devil Nephistopheles, and on the other side is Dr. Faust. For those who love chess, this particular portrait is very stimulating. For those who love human dynamics, this is a very engaging picture as you look into the faces of Nephistopheles and Dr. Faust. For those who understand the power and significance of spiritual warfare, you know this picture is far more than a game of chess between two people. It is a portrait illustrating good and evil. If you look into the eyes of Dr. Faust, you see a person who represents life. If you look into the eyes of Nephistopheles you see death, something evil and very wicked. You could spend the entire day observing the people as they study the famous painting and speculate on their thoughts.

A deeper look into the picture reveals that on Dr. Faust's side of the chess board, all of the pieces are gone except the king, the queen, and one little rook. Dr. Faust is worried, and you can see the smirk in the eyes of Nephistopheles. He knows he has Dr. Faust cornered. The end is near. Nephistopheles believes Dr. Faust does not have another move. It is now time for the kill. For some the game will be over. For others it appears life will end. It appears evil has been victorious over good.

Most tourists study the picture on average two minutes and then proceed on to the next portrait. One day, a very special tourist lingered longer. He was an international chess champion from Russia. You could see his brain racing. The king of chess saw what Nephistopheles and Dr. Faust didn't see. Suddenly, he shouted, "It's a lie!" Security guards approached him. He kept shouting, "It's a lie. It's a lie. The king has another move. The game is not over!"

Always remember with God all things are possible. The Lord always has another move.

Over My Dead Body

(Inspired by the late Reverend Samuel Proctor)

During segregation very few Black students were enrolled at Duke University. The Chaplain at the time, Dr. Howard Wilkerson, asked Samuel Proctor to speak in the chapel. Duke's president told Dr. Wilkerson that no Black would preach in that gothic church unless it was over his dead body. Two years later the president unexpectedly died. Dr. Wilkerson extended another invitation to Dr. Proctor to speak. While Samuel Proctor was reviewing his sermon he leaned over and asked Chaplain Wilkerson where the former president was buried. Wilkerson smiled at Proctor and said, "Directly under the pulpit." Proctor smiled and preached one of the best sermons of his life and stomped his feet the entire time.

My Daddy Is Coming Back

(Inspired by Reverend Jeremiah Wright, Jr.)

It was a beautiful summer afternoon in Chicago. If you ever want to see a beautiful waterway, Lake Michigan in the summertime is breathtaking. On this beautiful afternoon, a daughter's wish to spend more time with her father had come true. Throughout the week she had been pleading to spend time with her daddy. She complained that he spent more time with her brother, and not enough time with her. Today was going to be her day with just her and her daddy as they took the sailboat along Lake Michigan.

They had been out for almost an hour when unfortunately water began to pour through a hole in the bottom of the boat. Within minutes the father realized this was life threatening. He could swim, but his daughter could not. He had open heart surgery several months ago and was not strong enough to hold her while swimming. For a moment he didn't know what to do. He finally decided to swim back to shore and come back with the Coast Guard to save his baby girl.

He asked his daughter if she remembered how to float. "Sort of," she said, and for several minutes, the daughter practiced in front of her father. She turned over on her back and floated. Kicking her legs and extending her arms, she floated in a circle until the father felt confident that she would be okay while he swam ashore. The father swam ashore as fast as he could, only to find no Coast Guard and no boats. He flagged a taxi to Navy Pier, which was almost 50 blocks away. With a great sense of urgency, he informed the Coast Guard of the problem.

They immediately went out in the boat looking for his baby girl. They looked for almost two hours and there was no sign of her. The Coast Guard wanted to stop, due to darkness, but the father pleaded with them to look one more time. The Coast Guard agreed, but only to pacify him. Instead of finding her dead as they had assumed, she was floating on the water singing, "God will take care of you." They asked her, "How could you last this long?" "It was easy," she said. "My daddy said he was coming back for me, and my daddy never breaks his promises."

PART 5

FAMILY STORIES

If you want to study a people, observe their families.
How can a people build a nation if they can't build a family?
The state of the family is also
the state of the nation.

The Auction Story

Everybody in the community thought the husband and wife had it all. They had yachts, cars, limousines, mansions in several cities, and closets full of clothes. They had everything—except for a child. The father preferred a little boy.

Finally, the Lord blessed them in their 40s with their heart's desire and gave them a little boy. They were ecstatic and their lives were complete. At the tender age of seven, the little boy mysteriously died. The mother felt complete. She had experienced almost every materialistic possession and had been blessed with seven years with her son and shortly there afterwards she died. The father was all alone and because he knew they were in Heaven, he wanted to die and be with them again.

There was a large auction to sell off the assets of the estate. People from surrounding towns all came to bid on those luxurious items. It was as if a grand lottery had invaded the town. The auctioneer read the rules of the estate. The father required that the first item to be auctioned was the portrait of their little boy. The enthusiasm waned from the crowd. They did not want a portrait of a dead little boy. They had come all this way to bid on yachts, cars, clothes, mansions, and jewelry. No one bidded on the portrait, and the auctioneer returned to the podium and announced that the auction could not continue until the portrait had been bought. Finally, an elderly woman in the rear said, "Twenty dollars." The auctioneer said, "Twenty dollars once. Twenty dollars twice." No one countered. "Twenty dollars, sold to the woman in the rear."

The anticipation began to rise. Excitement was in the air. The people began to prepare their bids for the yachts, cars, clothes, mansions and jewelry. They waited impatiently for the auctioneer to return to the podium and auction the first item. The auctioneer said, "I regret to inform you, but the second rule of the estate is that the person who has my son gets everything else. The auction is now over. The lady in the rear receives the yachts, mansions, cars, clothes, and jewelry. She gets it all.'"

No Invitation

Today was the little boy's birthday, and he was excited. He didn't know what was going to happen. He was hoping his parents would give him a party. He didn't know what time the party would take place. He didn't know the location or who was going to attend. He thought about all the gifts he wanted. He dressed and went outside. His friends would probably slip and tell him about the surprise party. One boy told him it was going to take place at six-o'clock and it was going to be at his aunt's house. He ran home excited for he had finally secured the news.

It was December 25 and the party was going to be at six-o'clock. Everyone would be there with gifts. He was surprised that no one in his family had said anything. They didn't say how excited they were that he had been born or how much they loved him. Had it not been for his friend he never would have known. That bothered him, so he went to his bedroom. Deeply troubled, he fell into a deep sleep.

When he woke up, it was six-thirty; he had been asleep for several hours. The house was perfectly still. He got up and looked in the bedrooms. His parents weren't there, nor were his two brothers and two sisters. This was really going to be a surprise party. They even planned his nap. How did they know that he was going to take a nap on his birthday? He hurried and dressed and walked the three blocks to his aunt's house. Cars were parked everywhere. Children were coming from all over the community. He said to himself, "You would have thought it was Michael Jordan's or Michael Jackson's birthday. Everybody is here." December 25 was going to be a great day.

He tried to enter through the front door, but it was too crowded. He went around to the back door but to no avail. He looked through the basement window of his aunt's house and saw people dancing, eating, and playing games and having fun. He went around to the other side of the house and looked through the window, hoping he would be spotted. Maybe someone would open up the window and let him into his party to receive his gifts. Then they started giving gifts to each other. He seemed perplexed. "How can they give gifts to each other when it is my birthday?" he wondered. He put his hands on his hips and said, "Ain't this nothing. It is my birthday and I wasn't invited. They are having fun and I'm not even there. They are giving presents to each other." The little boy named Jesus walked home alone on December 25.

I'm Afraid of the Dark

(Inspired by Reverend Frederick Haynes III)

It had been a long, trying day for the father. He worked hard for ten hours, only to find out at the end of the day that the plant was relocating and that he would be out of a job after 30 days. As he was driving home, all he could think about was going home and having a good cry.

No sooner had he turned his key in the door his wife said, "It's your turn to read Denise a story and tuck her into bed." Then she said hello to him. He was not going to argue with his wife. He was going to read Denise a story, tuck her in, and then go to bed.

He went upstairs to the bedroom of his princess. "Hi, Daddy," she said, and all of his fatigue fell away, and he hugged his baby girl. She said, "Can you read me a story, Daddy?" He read a story and then she said, "Can you read me another story?" He was tired, but he read Denise another story. After he finished, he said, "Goodnight, baby girl."

He was about to turn off the light when Denise said, "I'm afraid of the dark. Can you stay here with me?" He went back to her bed. She reached for his hand and said, "Daddy, you have big hands." She put her hand inside his hand and said, "Daddy, see how big your hand is? Mine is small." And she told her Daddy, "Please don't leave me because I'm afraid of the dark." Slowly Denise began to fall asleep and the clutch of her hand on his hand began to slip.

Quietly, he got up, turned off the light, and went into his bedroom. Laying prostrate on the floor, he stretched out his hands and said, "Father, I am afraid of the dark. I'm putting it all in your hands."

Twins

Rudy and Randy were twins. People marveled at how identical they were to each other, and would ask their parents how they could tell them apart, especially when they dressed alike. The parents said, "It is difficult. They even sound alike, but they have two totally different personalities." And then they would tell them the following story:

One day they placed the children in two different rooms. They placed Rudy in a room that looked like a toy store. There were electronic and board games, books, balls, bats, skating boards, lego blocks, G.I. Joes, a basketball, a baseball, and a racing car set. This was a fantastic play room. The parents said, "In less than an hour, Rudy literally destroyed almost every toy and was completely bored and wanted to come out."

"We placed Randy in a room full of horse manure, and even though the smell was unbearable, Randy stayed there for hours. We wondered what could Randy be doing in a room full of horse manure. Finally we couldn't take it any longer. We opened the door and couldn't find Randy. I didn't want to go any further, but I knew Randy had to be there. I hollered and said, 'Randy where are you?' Randy said, 'There has to be a pony in here somewhere!'"

Mary's Husband

He was a pastor and a congressman. The church held him in high esteem, and his constituents referred to him as the "Honorable." His schedule was extremely demanding. During the week, he was in Washington representing his district. On the weekends, he was pastoring his flock.

One Sunday morning he noticed that his wife of more than 25 years appeared sad and melancholy. He asked her about it and she said, "Pastor and Mr. Honorable, you would not understand." With that, she went upstairs and cried.

He arrived at church that morning and asked three of his ministers to preach the three services. He took a two-week leave of absence from his church and from Congress. He flew to the mountains of Colorado and went on a 14-day fast. Slowly, he emptied himself. Humility was restored, and he became closer to God. He had talked with God for years, but seldom had he listened. He meditated on Genesis 2:24, "They shall become one flesh."

He arrived home to speak at a major citywide rally. He asked his wife to accompany him. As she had done for more than 25 years, she was there to support him. The host of the ceremony asked him before his speech if there was anything in particular he wanted said in the introduction.

He said, "Tell them I am Mary's husband!" The moderator did as requested. He stood up to speak and blew a kiss at his wife and whispered, "I finally understand."

A Mother's Love

She was a single parent with two children. She was on her way to work with her six-year-old daughter and her two-year-old son strapped in the back. Her daughter was to be dropped off at elementary school, and the son was on his way to pre-school. It was another typical day. She had awakened at five-o'clock in the morning, dressed by six, woke the children, dressed and fed them, and at six-forty-five she was out the door.

Later that evening, she would pick them up at six-o'clock, return home, make dinner, check homework, put them to bed, and repeat the process all over again—so she thought. Today was going to be an unusual day. As she drove along the lakefront, her car skidded and went into the river. Less than an hour later the rescue team arrived. It appeared the daughter died on impact. The mother was in an unusual position. She was still in the driver's seat, and the boy was over and above her. When the car hit the railing and went toward the water, she grabbed her son from the back seat and held him over her head. The cold water ultimately froze her. She held her son over her head and she died with her arms locked in that position. The rescue team was still talking about it as they rushed the boy to the hospital for tests.

Present

A father who had made the military his career would often impose that same strict regimen on his children. He would line his children up for roll call before they left home. Like a military officer, he would check his children to make sure their helmet, shield, and sword were in the proper position. He would require that they memorize a scripture before leaving home.

One day the father asked his nine-year-old son Victor to describe heaven. Victor stepped forward and said, "God will go through the attendance book like my teacher does at school and call out the names. He will say 'Daddy' and you will say 'present.' He will say 'Mommy' and she will say 'present.' He will say 'Victor' and I will say 'present.'" The father nodded in agreement and Victor stepped back into attention.

Several weeks later, Victor was the unfortunate victim of a drive-by shooting. He was fatally wounded. All of the family members, including aunts, uncles, and grandparents, gathered around his bedside. The doctor informed the family that Victor would probably not make it through the night. The family was distraught. One hour before he died, while he could not talk, he gestured to his father to bring a sheet a paper. His father helped him hold the pen and he scribbled with his father's assistance, "Present!"

Friends

Nicole was a beautiful sister. She was seventeen years old, starting guard on the basketball team, popular, and an honor roll student. Unfortunately, like Arthur Ashe, Nicole was a victim of a bad blood transfusion and was HIV positive for AIDS. This was supposed to be her shining year. Scholarships would be coming her way. Proms were right around the corner. She was looking forward to her graduation. Some of the girls on the basketball team wanted Nicole to resign because they thought if her sweat landed on the ball and they touched it, they'd catch the virus. In the cafeteria, the boys and girls who used to sit with her now stayed away from her.

Nicole decided to run for Senior Class President and her campaign speech was going to be "What It Means to be a Friend." The auditorium was packed to hear the seven presidential candidates. Nicole was the last speaker. You could almost hear a pin drop in the auditorium. Slowly, she walked to the podium. She said, "If I had given this speech one year ago I am certain you would have elected me president."

"One year ago, I thought you were my friends. I did not know the only reason you liked me was because I was the leading scorer on the basketball team, an honor roll student, and your homecoming queen. Today I stand before you, no longer on the basketball team, struggling to remain on the honor roll because I have missed several weeks of school, and no longer a beauty queen. I stand before you as your friend. Something very terrible has happened to me, but my feelings toward you have not changed. I stand before you as your friend, and I would like to have all of my friends who still care about me to please stand." You could hear a pin drop. Slowly, almost every student stood.

Gongie

I've never met a woman like my grandmother. I have never seen Jesus, but I believe I have seen Jesus in my grandmother. My grandmother never announced she knew the seven cardinal virtues of Maat or the seven principles of the Nguzo Saba. My grandmother lived them every day.

When I was an infant, my mother became very ill and because my father had to work, they made a decision to send me to Nacogdoches, Texas, to be with my grandmother whom we called Gongie. Several months later my mother regained her health and quite naturally wanted her son back in Chicago. Gongie had decided I belonged to her and literally every family member had to remind Gongie that she was not the biological mother and to return her grandson back to Chicago. The bond was set between me and my grandmother. I was her first grandchild. I visited her every summer after the end of each school year. She taught me Bible stories and took me to church on Wednesday and all day Sunday.

My grandmother worked at the cleaners and was paid meager wages, as low as $25 per week. On the night of my graduation, my grandmother not only attended the graduation ceremony in Chicago, she gave me $100. I looked at my parents in disbelief and cried. My grandmother looked surprised. How could someone make $25 per week, fly to Chicago, and give their grandson $100? How could the Lord feed 5,000 men, women, and children with five loaves and two fish? I can't wait to go to Heaven and see Jesus and Gongie.

I Love You "Soo" Much

I have a theory that some mothers raise their daughters and love their sons. They have double standards for their sons and daughters. They make their daughters come in early and not their sons. They make their daughters study and not their sons. They make their daughters do indoor chores and not their sons. They make their daughters go to church and not their sons.

I met a mother once who shared with me. She loved her son "soo" much that she was going to give him tough love. She was going to correct part of the problem with African American males by raising a responsible son. She decided that all the traits that she was looking for in a man she would develop in her son. She had numerous rules in her house. She told her son, "If you ever get locked up in jail don't even think about calling me to get you out." The son looked at her and said, "You would let me, your only son, stay in jail?" She looked back and said very sternly, "Yes I would."

Another rule was that he would always respect her regardless of his height, weight, muscles, and age. She said, "Don't ever think that because you are taller, heavier, and stronger that you can dominate me." She then looked him square in the eyes and said, "I love you 'soo' much I would go to jail for you." He looked at her as if he didn't understand. She looked right back and said, "If you ever put your hands on me, you will die and I will be in jail. I love you 'soo' much I would go to jail for you."

Talk To My Daddy

David skipped from his house to the park. He couldn't wait to get on the slide and the swings. He noticed a little boy playing in the sand box who looked very sad. David decided that before he played he would find out why the little boy was so sad.

David approached him and said, "What is your name?" The little boy said, "My name is Johnny." David then asked, "Why are you so sad?" Johnny said, "My daddy was laid off of his job yesterday and he is very sad. He told our family last night that he didn't know how we were going to stay in our house and have food to eat and then he began to cry. I had never seen my daddy cry before. I've never missed a meal, and I don't think all of us can fit into Granny's house."

David asked Johnny, "Where does your father work?" Johnny answered, "Brown's Manufacturing." David smiled and asked Johnny, "Do you mind if we go for a walk? There is somebody I want you to meet." Johnny shrugged his shoulders and said, "Okay." They walked eight blocks from the park and went inside this huge building, more than ten stories high. They walked right by the security guard and he did not stop David. They entered the elevator and went to the tenth floor. They exited the elevator, walked past another security guard and the secretary and entered into his father's office.

"Who is your friend?" David's father asked. David said, "His name is Johnny and we need to have a talk with you." Later the little boys walked from the office and went to Johnny's house. His father was sitting on the porch with his chin in his palms looking frustrated. Johnny ran to his father and said, "You have your job back! His daddy got your job back. They are not going to lay you off." The father looked at his son in disbelief and said, "How could this happen? Are you making this up?" Johnny looked at David and David looked at Johnny's father and said, "I talked to my Daddy."

The Burn

A baby was in her mother's arms, babbling and unable to speak a clear word. With most babies, their first words are Mama or Dada, but the infant girl kept pointing to the black mark on her mother's face. The mother was teaching the daughter to say burn, burn, burn, and the baby kept trying to say burn, burn, burn. As soon as the baby learned how to talk, the first thing she wanted to know was how her mother had gotten burned.

The mother sat the baby down and said, "There was a fire in the house and I was not leaving until I got you out of your room. A plank fell down on my face and burned my cheek. I didn't feel it when it first happened. I was so afraid that I was not going to get you out of your crib. It was only when I reached outside and had you in my arms that I realized I had been burned. They took me to the hospital and did everything they could, but said the mark would be permanent." The baby looked at her mother and said, "You did that for me?" The mother looked at the daughter and said, "I'd do it all over again, even if it meant getting a burn on the other cheek."

We Forgot To Tell Him

The doctors met with the parents right after the birth of their son and said, "Congratulations on the birth of your son. Unfortunately. . . ."

The parents looked at each other in anguish for what they thought was going to be good news just turned bad. The doctor continued and said, "Your son was born with minor brain damage. We are going to keep him for some additional tests. Our judgment is that he will never be able to utilize his full brain capacity. He will be able to learn but it will be at a much slower rate."

Twenty-two years later, the baby, now a young man, graduated from North Carolina A&T with a degree in chemical engineering. How did he do it? For some reason, his parents forgot to tell him that he would have to work harder on his spelling words and that he would need to begin studying on Tuesday for Friday's tests. They also forgot to tell him why he had to go to summer school every year.

They forgot to tell him why he took the SAT in his sophomore, junior, and senior years. His first score was 700, but his last was 1200. They forgot to tell him that he would be better off going to a junior college than one of the best engineering schools in the country. How unfortunate they forgot to tell him all of this, but then, does it really matter?

You Are A Robertson

(Inspired by the late Reverend Samuel Proctor)

Darnell Robertson was so excited about his 16th birthday. His father was steeped in tradition. His father and grandfather were both graduates of Morehouse and pastors. His mother and his grandmother were both doctors and graduates of Spelman. He had heard a lot over the years about generational blessings versus generational curses. Over the years he had been reminded on numerous occasions when he was acting up in church, "You should know better. You are a Robertson." When he was younger, his friends would look at him and he would look strange as adults would remind him, "You are a Robertson." It seemed like every time someone told him that, it always messed up whatever fun he was having.

In the Robertson family there was a tradition that you could not have your first date until you were sixteen years of age. Tonight was the night and he could not wait. He also was going to seriously think about whether he was going to maintain the Robertson tradition, attend Morehouse, and become a pastor. He was going to enjoy his first date. He regretted that some of his friends had already been dating for more than two years. But again, because he was a Robertson, he had to wait.

He was almost out the door when his father called him back and said, "You are a Robertson and there is a way to act on a date." He knew then the evening was spoiled. He knew then that he would have to be in at a certain time. He was going to have to treat his date a certain way. Kissing, hugging, and doing a "little sumthin sumthin" in the back seat was not what Robertson's do. He listened to his dad spoil the evening. He left the house, frustrated and knowing that throughout the evening, he would constantly hear in his mind, "You are a Robertson." He laughed to himself and said, "When I have children, I'm going to tell them the same thing."

Nosy Miss Jones from the Village

Raynard had it all planned this fall afternoon. School was only a half-day for staff development, and he and his girlfriend Renee were going to visit his house after school. No one would be home, and he and Renee would finally get a chance to make love. They were 14 years old, and they had been waiting an awfully long time. He had not told his parents about the half day of school, and he intercepted the reminder that had arrived in the mail.

He was halfway up the steps to his house with Renee when nosy Miss Jones stuck her head out the window and said, "You're home mighty early, Raynard. Does your Mama know you are home? Does your Mama know your girlfriend is going in the house without her being there?" Raynard knew he couldn't lie. If he lied she was going to call her, and if he told the truth she was going to call her. Miss Jones then told Raynard and Renee, "Sit down. I'm calling your Mama right now."

Raynard said he could have killed Miss Jones that day. Why did she have to stick her head out? Why didn't she mind her own business? Raynard knew that once his Mama received the call, she would be home in minutes, and he would not be able to sit down for the rest of the day. Raynard couldn't stand Miss Jones that day. Little did he know that that was the day she saved his life. Satan had planned for Raynard and Renee to make a baby that day. God and Miss Jones had different plans.

Blind Date in Cyberspace

Frederick lived in San Diego, and Marie lived in Boston. They met almost six months ago in cyberspace. They both had responded to a message board on the African American Images Web Page. They respected each other's comments and views on affirmative action, the welfare bill, economic empowerment, and other topics that were provided for readers to respond. They decided to continue their dialogue privately. They began e-mailing each other. This went on for several months, and they continued to appreciate each other's views and enjoy each other's company as best you can while in cyberspace.

Frederick often teased Marie about beautiful winters in San Diego and how harsh the winters were in Boston. They marveled at their closeness while living cross country. Frederick asked Marie if she would visit one February weekend to get away from the cold. He offered to split the airfare and hotel while she was in town. They agreed on the date and waited with great anticipation. They had talked and felt they knew each other, but they had never seen each other. He didn't know if she was tall or short, thin or heavy, pretty or ugly nor she about him. Early in the game they had agreed not to discuss looks.

The plan was that Frederick would have a name tag on his lapel so that when Marie got off the plane, she would recognize him.

Marie decided that she wanted to make it a little more interesting, so she asked her mother to come with her. When it was time to exit the plane, Marie told her mother, "Why don't you go out first and look for a man with a name tag that says, 'Frederick.' Tell him that you are Marie, and strike up a conversation about worldly issues because Frederick can talk about anything. I will wait until everyone has gotten off the plane to get off. If you tell me he is okay, then I'll come over to you."

Marie's mother exited the plane and approached Frederick—who turned out to be twenty-three, six-feet-two inches, 190 pounds, and very handsome. Marie's mother approached him and said, "Hi Frederick. We finally have a chance to see each other." Frederick smiled and looked at Marie's mother and said, "I've thought about you for months and I'm glad you arrived safely. I have all kinds of plans for us while you are here." Marie then exited the plane. Her mother gave her the nod. She walked over to them and said, "Hi, Frederick. My name is also Marie. This is my mother and we both came to see you."

No More Sheets

(Inspired by Reverend Juanita Bynum)

I was in Raleigh, North Carolina. I had just completed a keynote address to the Hayti community on my book *Restoring the Village: Solutions for the Black Family*. The speech concluded at eight-thirty. I signed books for more than an hour and Allison, one of the coordinators who lived close to the hotel, was driving me back to the hotel. It was a beautiful Friday evening. She drove a black Porsche and dressed in a sexy black leather jumpsuit. I politely asked her during our drive to the hotel what she planned to do for the rest of the evening. I had previously told her that I was going for a swim and the steam room and prepare for an early flight. She had already told me she was saved, well educated, and gainfully employed.

She told me, "I'm going to do almost the same. I am going to take a hot bubble bath, read my Bible, and make love to Jesus. I am tired of playing games. I couldn't have told you this a year ago. My legs were in South Carolina, my heart was in Georgia, my breasts in Virginia, and my mind in New York. The brothers had me going. They had me believing I was not complete without them, especially on weekends. The Lord told me 'You have filled yourself with everyone but me. You have 'deposits' from men but not with me. How can you marry when you are not single?' I am a full woman now. I am complete with or without a man. The next time somebody gets my legs, heart, and mind, they will have to love my Jesus."

It's A Set Up

It was two o'clock in the morning in New York City. The prominent Black politician was running for the Presidency. He had been campaigning all day in New York and had not fallen asleep until just after midnight. It had been a great day. He wanted to be the first African American President and New York was a critical state.

His sleep was interrupted with a knock on the door. He thought it was a mistake, but they kept knocking. He got out of bed and walked to the door. He looked through the peephole and opened the door. He was dressed in a T-shirt and had pulled on a pair of pants. There standing before him was a beautiful woman dressed in a satin red robe. She was Halle Berry, Tyra Banks, and more. She asked if she could come in and talk.

He looked at her and considered his options. He could bring her in and enjoy the rest of the evening. He could tell her that he was married and had been for more than 30 years. He could tell her that he was saved, washed by the blood, and because of his relationship with Jesus Christ couldn't let her come into his room. He could tell her about the hidden camera behind the wall. If he let her in, the FBI would come knocking on his door five minutes later and his whole career would go down the tube. So he looked at her, smiled, and said, "It's a set up. Keep hope alive. I love you very much" and closed the door.

I Will Never Leave You

They were a beautiful couple. Everybody in church and the neighborhood raved about them. They had a boy and a girl. They all loved each other. It appeared to be a marriage made in heaven. One day the husband left. He did not give a reason. She asked herself, "Was there any sign? Didn't you know? Didn't you see something on the wall? Is he involved with someone else? Is he on drugs? Was he depressed? Is he no longer in relationship with the Lord?"

She couldn't answer any of those questions. She used to love her house. Her house was also a home but now she hated coming home, hated the reminders of him, wondered if he would ever come back. She disliked it when the children asked her, "Where is Daddy? Did you run him away? Did we run him away?"

She became depressed. She talked with her saved girlfriend at lunch, and they prayed. Her girlfriend told her, "He is waiting at home for you right now. You need to leave work early and go home." She ran out of the door and hollered to her girlfriend, "Please tell my boss that I had to go home early."

As she frantically caught a bus home, she wondered how her girlfriend knew that he would be home today. She made it home in record breaking time and opened the door. There was a peace in the house that she hadn't felt since her husband left. She began to walk through the house, looking for her husband.

A small voice said, "Sit on the sofa." She obediently sat and anxiously waited. The voice began to talk. "You came home looking for him when you should have come home looking for me. I am your first love. I promised the moment you loved me that I would never leave you nor forsake you. Dry your eyes and give me all your tears and all your pain, my child. Before the evening is over, I will answer all of your questions. I will tell you the status of your husband. I will remind you of the covenant we have with each other. Your pain will end tonight. You must promise that you will never place anyone before me again."

I Made Him

It had been a great thirty-year high school reunion. They were in the car driving home. They had seen many old friends. Most of their classmates had done very well. Everyone seemed to have gained a little weight, and lost a little hair, but by and large, everyone seemed to be in great spirits. Donald teased Tiffany and said, "You're lucky to have a husband like me. President of the largest Black bank in America. Did you see your old boyfriend? Overweight and shining shoes at the barber shop. Next time you are on my last nerve I'm going to drop you off at your old boyfriend's house and see if he can do for you like I have."

Tiffany looked at him and said, "Oh really. So you really think you're all that? You didn't know if I had married Stan he too would have been the president of the bank and would be driving me home. Heaven forbid where you would be. It had nothing to do with you."

Hot Fur in the Summertime

(Inspired by the late Reverend Samuel Proctor and contributed by Reverend Ozzie Smith)

One warm Sunday in July during service, the pastor of the church could not help but notice that one of his parishioners was oddly dressed for the climate. The parishioner was wearing a full length mink coat with a matching mink hat in the dead heat of summer. Preaching became quite a chore as he tried to say a word while seeing the shock and staring faces of the other members. "Hot Fur!" the people whispered during the sermon. It was quite annoying as he could no more stop preaching than they could stop whispering. Eventually the sermon ended. The invocation extended and the benediction was given.

The preacher hurried to his study and was followed by an entourage of curious congregants. "Did you see that?" was on their lips, but before they could ask the question, there came a knock on the door of the pastor's study. "Come in," he said. In came the parishioner who wore the hot fur coat. She immediately began to reveal her bill of particulars. There was crypt silence and she began to tell the story.

"I am sure that all of you are wondering why on earth I would wear such a hot coat on this very hot day. Well, my husband came home drunk again last night. He passed out in bed. When I arose this morning to come to church, he awakened in a rage, saying that he would not allow me to worship today. I had to run out of the bedroom in my pajamas as he chased me as best he could. He yelled, 'So that you can't go to church I've locked all of your Sunday clothes in the trunk of my car!'"

"I ran toward the kitchen, remembering the old print duster that I wear on Saturdays to clean our home. I quickly put it on and ran to the hall closet where this fur coat was hanging. Maybe he thought that I would not wear it, but was he ever wrong. I did not want any of you to see the duster, so I covered it up with this coat. I just had to hear a word from the Lord today by anyway I could. I thank God for the word today because it will sustain me as I return to the Hell that I have been living with."

Forgiven

She was frantically running down the street. She had eight more blocks before she finally made it to the hospital. The nurse had just called her and told her that her father was dying. They hadn't spoken in several years. The memory of the day her mother and father broke up was still on her mind. For a long time she hated her father for breaking up their beautiful home, and she blamed alcohol as the major culprit. She made a vow she would never touch alcohol.

She finally made it to the hospital. Unfortunately, he had passed. A sheet had been pulled over his face. She pleaded with the doctor, "Please bring him back, please bring him back." She pounded on her chest. "I never got a chance to tell him after he left that I still loved him. I never told him that I understand that it was not him but the alcohol. Please bring him back. How will he ever know that I love him? How will he ever know that I forgave him?"

She was crying. The nurse walked over to her and said, "This was a note your father dictated before he died." She wiped her eyes and began to read the note. "I am sorry I couldn't wait for you, my love. I know that you are on the way. If I only had one word to tell you it would be 'forgiven.'"

Midnight

He was scheduled to be executed in the next 72 hours. The conversation seemed to be going in two different directions. The son kept telling his father, "I didn't do it. They have the wrong man. I didn't do it, Daddy, I didn't do it." The father kept asking the son, "Do you believe Jesus Christ is your Lord and Savior? Are you willing to confess with your mouth and believe with your heart?" The son told his father, "I don't believe in God. God does not exist. If there truly was a God I would not be in this jail cell and I would not be waiting for execution. If there was a God then the real killer would have been caught." He then turned away from his father angrily and went back to his jail cell.

Three days later he was executed and unfortunately a week later the real killer was captured. The chaplain had given the father his son's remains including the Bible his father had given him. Months later the father opened the Bible and found these words, "They may have my body, but Jesus has my soul. It was midnight when I met the Lord for myself."

An Adoption Reunion

George and Michael were in their 40s. They had relocated to Flint, Michigan, where they met each other while working at General Motors. They had been there about a year, both had families, and were looking for a house. They enjoyed each other's company so much that they decided to look for a house in the same subdivision. Fortunately they were both able to find houses for their families and they continued to enjoy each other's company.

One day while they were fishing, George and Michael began talking about their past. George mentioned that he had been put up for adoption when he was less than two years old in Seattle. Michael listened. The story sounded so familiar because he too had been placed for adoption in Seattle when he was less than one year old. Slowly, it began to dawn on them both that they were brothers. Each knew he had a sibling, but had given up looking for each other because the adoption agency would not provide any information. Tears fell uncontrollably. They hugged each other. This was truly a miracle. Only God can explain how almost 40 years later and more than 3,000 miles they were reunited.

The Treasure

(contributed by Alice Gray)

The cheerful girl with bouncy golden curls was almost five. Waiting with her mother at the checkout stand, she saw them: a circle of glistening white pearls in a pink foil box.

"Oh please, Mommy. Can I have them? Please, Mommy, please!"

Quickly the mother checked the back of the little foil box and then looked back into the pleading blue eyes of her little girl's upturned face.

"A dollar ninety-five. That's almost $2. If you really want them, I'll think of some extra chores for you and in no time you can save enough money to buy them for yourself. Your birthday's only a week away and you might get another crisp dollar bill from Grandma."

As soon as Jenny got home, she emptied her penny bank and counted out 17 pennies. After dinner, she did more than her share of chores and she went to the neighbor and asked Mrs. McJames if she could pick dandelions for ten cents. On her birthday, Grandma did give her another new dollar bill and at last she had enough money to buy the necklace.

Jenny loved her pearls. They made her feel dressed up and grown up. She wore them everywhere—Sunday school, kindergarten, even to bed. The only time she took them off was when she went swimming or had a bubble bath. Mother said if they got wet, they might turn her neck green.

Jenny had a very loving daddy and every night when she was ready for bed, he would stop whatever he was doing and come upstairs to read her a story. One night when he finished the story, he asked Jenny, "Do you love me?"

"Oh, yes, Daddy. You know that I love you."

"Then give me your pearls."

"Oh, Daddy, not my pearls. But you can have Princess—the white horse from my collection. The one with the pink tail. Remember, Daddy? The one you gave me. She's my favorite."

"That's okay, Honey. Daddy loves you. Good night." And he brushed her cheek with a kiss.

About a week later, after the story time, Jenny's daddy asked again, "Do you love me?"

"Daddy, you know I love you."

"Then give me your pearls."

"Oh, Daddy, not my pearls. But you can have my baby doll. The brand new one I got for my birthday. She is so beautiful and you can have the yellow blanket that matches her sleeper."

"That's okay. Sleep well. God bless you, little one. Daddy loves you." And as always, he brushed her cheek with a gentle kiss.

A few nights later when her daddy came in, Jenny was sitting on her bed with her legs crossed Indian-style. As he came close, he noticed her chin was trembling and one silent tear rolled down her cheek.

"What is it, Jenny? What's the matter?"

Jenny didn't say anything but lifted her little hand up to her daddy. And when she opened it, there was her little pearl necklace. With a little quiver, she finally said, "Here, Daddy. It's for you."

With tears gathering in his own eyes, Jenny's kind daddy reached out with one hand to take the dime-store necklace, and with the other hand he reached into his pocket and pulled out a blue velvet case with a strand of genuine pearls and gave them to Jenny. He had had them all the time. He was just waiting for her to give up the dime-store stuff so he could give her genuine treasure.

So like our heavenly Father.

PART 6

Nguzo Saba

the seven principles of Kwanzaa

And

Maat

the seven cardinal virtues

A people without positive values are dangerous. We struggle not with flesh and blood, but people without positive values.

Learning New Math

I was an excellent math student. I used to receive 100s on almost all of my quizzes and tests. I was very disappointed when I received less than 100. One day in class, after looking at my paper, another 100, I asked my best friend Darryl what he received. "Forty," he said, and I laughed. A couple other classmates around me laughed as well.

Mrs. Butler pointed at me with her finger and gestured for me to come up to her desk. She asked me my grade on my math test? I smiled and said, "You know what I received. I always receive 100." She then asked me to bring my paper up to her desk. I went back to my desk and retrieved the paper and brought it back to her desk. She put an "X" through my hundred with a red pen. I was furious. I didn't know if I wanted to strangle her, cry, or both. She then asked Darryl to come up to her desk with his paper. She asked Darryl what grade he received? He embarrassingly said, "40." She then looked at me and said, "From now on whatever grade Darryl receives will also be your grade."

I never laughed at Darryl's scores again. Darryl and I worked math problems before school, during recess, and after school. This was my best school year. I learned more than mathematics. I learned to whom much is given much is required, and what you do to the least of these you also do to Him.

Price or Principle?

(Inspired by Reverend Jeremiah Wright, Jr.)

It was going to be another intellectually stimulating class in ethics. There were 30 students in the class, and one of the most brilliant minds in the country lecturing. The professor was thought provoking and his students felt involved and engaged in the process. The professor asked "Would you have sex once with this person for $1 million? The person is healthy and has no sexually transmitted diseases. Write on your paper yes or no." Twenty of the students said no. The remaining ten said yes.

Later the professor lowered the price from $1 million to $500,000, then to $100. Finally, one of the students who answered yes said, "What do you think I am, a prostitute?" The professor immediately responded and said, "That was confirmed when you said yes. The only thing we are trying to resolve now is the price." He concluded the class by saying, "Price over Principle equals Prostitute."

A Twenty-Dollar Bill

(Inspired by Reverend Jesse Jackson, Sr.)

Jesse Jackson, Sr., his brother Noah, and his father cleaned offices in Greenville, South Carolina. Jim Crow was alive and well. Black people could clean the office at night, but not work in the office during the day. There were many offices to clean and very little time to complete them.

Jesse could never understand why people thought that Black people were so filthy and White people were so clean. All you had to do was clean their offices or homes to see their sloppiness. But that was not the only lesson Jesse learned while cleaning Mr. Charlie's office. Strategically located in various offices would be $20 bills. During that era that's about all they were paid for the entire job. The first time Jesse saw a $20 bill he wanted to keep it. He told his Daddy, "Look what I found. A $20 bill." His father looked at him and said, "Son, where did you find that?" Jesse said, "On the oak desk." His father told Jesse to "put the $20 back, it is not yours." Jesse pleaded with his father to let him keep it. His father said, "You don't understand, son. They want you to take it and accuse you of stealing. This is the bait and we are not biting."

A View from the Top

He had been trying so hard to reach the top. He wanted his song and CD to reach platinum. He desired to grace the cover of major magazines. He sought to win every prize at the major musical awards.

She averaged 27 points per game and had been the scoring champ for the past three years. Her team had won three WNBA championships. They were reaching for the top. Each one climbed one side of the mountain.

They both reached the top at the same time, only to find out there was nothing there. They looked at each other and said, "Is this it? We worked this hard and this is all the glory?" They both began to look down. They saw so many people they had stepped over and taken advantage of to reach the top.

They also saw so many people who wanted to be in their position. They looked around and saw friends, idols, and role models who had fallen into drugs, depression, and immoral living. People at the bottom kept asking, "I don't understand, they had everything." They realized there was still something missing at the top. Before they could figure it out, they were interrupted by the Lord who said, "You fool. Tonight I come for you."

PART 7

COLLEGE

*There is no group of Africans in the world
with more college degrees than African
Americans, but educated to do what? and
for whom?*

Tuskegee University

Tuskegee is considered one of the best Black colleges in the country, producing some of the finest engineers, architects, and veterinarians. But it wasn't always that way.

It was 1872 and Booker T. Washington, who had taught himself how to read as a young child, at the age of 16 was walking from West Virginia to Hampton, Virginia, on his way to college. He had a tremendous desire to learn and was determined to receive a college education. Booker T. Washington had no money and worked as a janitor to pay most of his expenses. Four years later, he graduated with honors and distinguished himself by giving the commencement address.

He so impressed his teachers and college administrators that five years later, the president of Hampton University recommended Booker T. Washington to be the first president of the newly formed university in Tuskegee, Alabama. When he took over in 1881, the school had a budget of $2,000 and a few acres of land. When he died in 1915, Tuskegee had more than 60 buildings, an endowment of nearly $3 million, and more than two thousand students.

The Wizard of Tuskegee

George Washington Carver was born in Diamond Grove, Missouri, in 1864. He worked his way through Simpson and Iowa State colleges and completed his masters degree. He accepted a position with Iowa University in Iowa City, the first African American to do so. He received a letter from Booker T. Washington asking to join him as they would work together to educate Blacks in the South. George Washington Carver left the comforts and prestige of Iowa University and arrived in Tuskegee, Alabama, where there was little money, few scientific resources, but two men with a vision.

George Washington Carver inspired his students and continued to do research. He helped farmers around the region to rotate their crops, showing them the importance of replenishing the soil. He developed more than 325 products from the peanut and sweet potato. Presidents called him their friend. Scientists from around the world sought his advice and opinion.

In the early 1900s, Thomas Edison offered to pay him $100,000 to work in a laboratory designed to his specifications if he would leave Tuskegee. Henry Ford matched that figure and offered him a job with the Ford Motor Company. Can you imagine what $100,000 would be worth in today's figures?

How many African American professors would stay at Black colleges if they were offered that kind of money at White universities? I wonder how many African American professionals would stay with an African American company if they were offered substantially more at a White firm? George Washington Carver chose to stay and was committed to empowering Black people in the South. He thought he could be of greater service at Tuskegee. When he died, he was buried next to his friend, Booker T. Washington.

Mary McLeod Bethune

What can you do with $1.50? What can you do with five loaves and two fish? What can you do with a garbage dump? Mary McLeod Bethune was educated at Scotia Seminary in Concord, North Carolina. The Lord inspired her to attend Moody Bible Institute. She had planned to be a missionary in Africa.

Bethune found out that railroads were being built in Florida and was gravely concerned about the large number of young people who needed an education, and the lack of resources, facilities, and institutions to accommodate them. She took all that she had, which was $1.50, to Daytona Beach, Florida, and used it as a down payment on a garbage dump. People only saw $1.50, a garbage dump, and a crazy woman who had a dream. Mary McLeod Bethune saw the Lord, and over a decade later, she saw 600 students, 32 teachers, property worth more than $1 million, and a merger between Bethune College and the Cookman Institute that now graduates 1,000 students per year.

Southern Mississippi University

How can a person who earns 50 cents per bundle washing and ironing clothes contribute $250,000 to a university? There are people who earn $100,000 per year and can't make a contribution of $5,000.

This woman's name is Oseola McCarty, and she lives in Hattiesburg, Mississippi. She always had a desire to go to school and receive an education, but unfortunately, at the end of sixth grade, she had to drop out of school to take care of her aunt. She washed and ironed clothes. Her starting rate for one week's bundle was 50 cents, and over the years it increased to $10.

In 1947, when she first started working, Southern Mississippi did not allow Blacks to attend SMU. Jim Crow was alive and well. She contributed $250,000 to the university to create the Oseola McCarty scholarship for needy students. It was the largest gift by an African American to a Mississippi university. This gift so inspired the nation that pledges came in from the entire country to match her pledge. This humble woman said, "Years ago my race couldn't go to that college, but now they can. The only thing I regret is that I didn't have more to give."

Anonymous Gift

(Inspired by the late Reverend Samuel Proctor)

When I was a young student at Virginia Union in 1940-1942, an anonymous philanthropist in New Hampshire paid my $100 tuition. I supposed the school thought that if I knew my benefactor's name I would write him to express my thanks and respectfully ask for more! And no doubt I would have. Sixteen years later, I was sitting in my office as President of the same school facing a distraught premed honor student in the senior class. He was a married veteran with two children and the bottom had dropped out of his life. He was telling me that he was stone broke. His rent was overdue, his children had been sick, and he had to give up. He already had been accepted to medical school, but he said there was no way he could attend.

As we pondered the problem the door opened and Mrs. Little, my ever present assistant, came in. "Sorry to interrupt," she said, "but I think you'll want to take this call." "I am terribly busy," I said, "can I call back?" "I think you should take it now," said Mrs. Little. A cracked voice came on the line.

"Are you the same Samuel Proctor who went to school at Virginia Union back in the 1940s?" "I am the same," I said. "I am the one who paid your tuition. I called to tell you that I am satisfied that I made a wise investment. I am pleased with your progress." I was dazed and I thanked him profusely.

He said, "Can you find me another student that I can help? I don't have much time left. I would like to do again what I did in your case." "Sir," I said with an involuntary tremor in my voice, "he is sitting in front of me as we speak." This was as close to a miracle as I have ever seen with the infinite probability that no human could ever align random events with such precision. There must be a God somewhere! I handed the phone to my student and left the room. I have no idea what they talked about, but when he came out of my office several minutes later, I was crying, Ms. Little was in tears, and the student, now the fabulous Dr. Charles Cummings, a prominent Richmond specialist in internal medicine, was smiling through his tears.

Building the Temple

It had been a long night for the eight-year-old little girl. She had suffered with asthma almost her entire life. The family had gathered throughout the week because, the doctors said she may not make it through the night. Unfortunately, the doctors were correct. When family members were preparing to take her to the morgue they looked beneath her pillow and found a small little note and a bag with 57 pennies. The note said, "Use this to help build the little temple so more children can go to school."

The following Sunday, the pastor told the story and the congregation responded. The newspapers nationwide picked up the story. The offerings began to come in to build the little temple. That temple now seats 3,300 people in its main sanctuary. It also built a school called Temple University, which blossomed into Temple Hospital. All of this started with a little girl, a note, and 57 pennies.

Mr. President

A small Western college was struggling financially. The buildings were shabby, and staff salaries were meager. A stranger visited the campus one day and asked a man who was washing a wall where he could find the president. "I think you can see him at his house at noon," was the reply. The visitor went as directed and met the president. He recognized him as the same man who was scrubbing the wall earlier in the day, though he was now in different clothes.

Later that week, a letter came with a gift of $50,000 for the college. The spirit of service on the part of the president had made a positive impression on the visitor. Because the benefactor saw a man who was not too proud to help where needed, even though it involved what some might term a menial task, he was moved to contribute generously to the school.

The Power of Prayer

David was excited about going to college. He wanted to become a computer engineer. He had heard about the tremendous shortage of computer engineers and wanted to make a difference, not only for his race but for the nation. There was only one minor problem. He did not have any money. His parents kept reminding him that faith is the substance of things hoped for, the evidence of things unseen. They kept telling him to call those things that do not exist as if they were. David's parents kept saying, "We're praying for you." It must have been contagious because the pastor, deacons, and members would say the same thing, "We're praying for you."

David felt it would have been a lack of faith for him not to go the hundred miles to the state university to enroll in college, even though he thought it was futile to register with no money. He kept hearing his parents say, "We are praying for you." Things went well during registration. He was able to secure all of his classes on the days and times that he wanted, and he was even allowed to take an engineering class in his freshman year because of his excellent test scores in math and science.

Then came the real test of faith—the cashier's line. Fortunately, there were 30 to 40 students ahead of him, and he had time to pray. He thought about telling them he was available for work study. He knew not to ask about grants, that money dried up years ago. It amazed him how the country could find money to build prisons, but could not find money for needy college students. He decided he would plead with the cashier and promise to pay the bill before the end of the year. The line continued to move and he was next.

His palms began to sweat. He presented his registration form to the cashier. She looked at him and smiled and stamped "PAID IN FULL." He couldn't believe it. He ran to the nearest phone booth to call his parents. He said, "You wouldn't believe what they just did. They stamped on the registration 'PAID IN FULL.' I didn't give them any money. They didn't ask about a loan. They didn't mention work study." Mama was on one line and Daddy was on the other and they said, "We've been praying for you."

An Ungrateful College Student

A young man was preparing to graduate from college and for many months he had admired a beautiful sports car. His father promised it would be his graduation present. Finally, on the morning of his graduation, his father called him into his study. His father told him how proud he was to have such a fine son and told him how much he loved him. He handed his son a beautifully wrapped gift box. Curiously and somewhat disappointed, the son opened the box and found a lovely leather bound Bible with the young man's name embossed in gold. Angrily he raised his voice to his father and said, "With all of your money you gave me a Bible?" and he stormed out of the house.

Many years passed and the young man was very successful in business. He had a beautiful home and a wonderful family. He had not seen his father since graduation. He received a telegram informing him that his father had passed away. He went home immediately. When he arrived at his father's house, sadness and regret filled his heart.

He began to search through his father's important papers and saw the new Bible he had left years ago. With tears in his eyes he opened the Bible and began to turn the pages. His father had carefully underlined a verse, Matthew 7:11, "If you then being evil, know how to give good gifts to your children, how much more will your Father who is in heaven give good things to those who ask him." As he read those words, a car key dropped from the back of the Bible. On the tag was the date of his graduation and the words "PAID IN FULL."

Yale University

"How could you go out like that?" he asked. "You know better. You taught me about Ausar, Aset, and Heru. You taught me about Osiris, Isis, and Horus. You were the one that taught me the relationship between Maat, the Negative Confessions, and the Ten Commandments. How could someone like you, who is so Africentric, believe something so foolish as Jesus was born of virgin conception and that when He died, all of our sins were washed away? That He rose three days later and that we have the gift of eternal life? How could you believe that? You can't prove it. It is not scientific."

I asked the student from Yale to tell me about his family. I asked him about his father. He became a little irritated and said that his father left him when he was two years old and that he hasn't seen him since and doesn't want to see him. I then asked if his father was saved. He said "no."

I then asked him about his mother. You could see the smile in his eyes. He said, "My Mama is the best. It cost almost $30,000 to attend Yale and they only gave me $15,000 in grants, loans, and work study. My Mama pays the difference." "Your mother must have a very good job and a college degree," I said. He shrugged his head and said, "No, unfortunately my Mama does not have a degree. She works two jobs. She cleans houses during the day and hotels at night." I then asked him, "How do you think your mother does that? How do you think your mother raised you by herself? How do you think your mother has been able to work two jobs for over a decade? How do you think your mother was able to save $15,000?" Before he could answer, I asked, "Is your mother saved?" He said, "Yes. She prays for me all of the time."

The University of Chicago

(Inspired by Reverend Jeremiah Wright, Jr.)

They were finally going to resolve the issue. The big debate was going to take place. The best scholars from around the world were going to come together from Oxford, Harvard, Yale, Princeton, Stanford, Duke, the University of Chicago, and other schools to finally answer the question, "Is God Real?" The debate was open to the public. Following would be a brief question and answer period. For three hours scholars debated the big questions. "Is God real? How did the world begin? Who developed the world? How did life begin? Who is in control of the stars, moon, and sun? Is Heaven and Hell real? Where are the three days between Good Friday and Easter Sunday? Is Satan real? Has the Bible been tampered with? If God is real, why is the world in such turmoil?"

Finally, three hours later, they opened the floor for questions. The first person who asked a question did not fit the prototype of the audience. He was not a student or a professor at a prestigious school. He was an elderly Black man, poorly dressed, and rudely chomping on an apple while he spoke. As he asked his question, he continued chomping on the apple. He asked the distinguished panel, "The apple that I just ate, was it bitter or sweet?" The panel had the unmitigated gall to think they could answer the question. The elderly man walked away from the microphone commenting, "only when you have tasted Him for yourself, when you know what He has done for you, will you be able to answer my question."

Morgan State 1973

I was on the track and debate teams at Illinois State. I had just completed my sophomore year and the Lord touched me and inspired me to do something different with my collegiate career. My younger sister was going to attend Illinois State and I wanted her to have her own personality and life experiences. I always wanted to go to a Black college and this was an opportunity to go on the exchange program. Illinois State had an exchange program with Towson State, which is in a Baltimore suburb. Towson had an exchange program with Morgan State, which is a Black college in Baltimore.

Unfortunately, housing at Towson was limited, and the housing department arranged to have me stay off campus with a local family. At the time I had a European name and the family thought that I was White. When they saw me at their front steps, luggage in hand, they realized their mistake. They increased the rent 100 percent and rather than a room on the second floor I was now being ushered to the attic. They knew these new arrangements were unacceptable. I left their house and went back to Towson and was allowed to stay in a dormitory room because school had not opened.

I cried that night to the Lord and reminded Him that like the Israelites, it would have been better if we had just stayed in Egypt and Illinois State rather going to Baltimore with no place to stay. The Lord listened and absorbed all my tears. The next morning He inspired me to look in the Yellow Pages for juvenile delinquent centers. He told me to call them and let them know I was a positive Black male role model and in exchange for room and board, I would mentor and tutor their boys. The director said he had never done that before but it sounded like a good idea. He granted me an interview. He was impressed with me and agreed to the arrangement. The boys, ages seven to thirteen, lived on the first two floors, and I resided on the third floor.

Ironically, after my interview, the director accepted two other men in the community, and one of them became my best friend. The juvenile delinquent center was literally right in the middle between Morgan and Towson. Mentoring the boys gave me the idea to write my bestseller *Countering the Conspiracy to Destroy Black Boys.*

I ran track at Towson and became a vegetarian. One fall Friday evening, with no homework, God sent me to the library. That night I read the *Autobiography of Malcolm X* and *Who Needs the Negro.* I became committed to the liberation of Black people and legally changed my name that year.

PART 8

NATURE

*Never become so busy that you don't listen
to the birds, enjoy the warmth of the sun,
walk along the water, and appreciate the
gifts of God.*

Collective Leadership

One of the ways I measure a good leader is by assessing the strength of the number two person. Would the organization function if the leader was not present? Insecure leaders make it difficult for the number two person to grow to their full potential.

I have had the privilege of observing geese fly south for the winter. It is amazing to see them fly. It is majestic the way they fly so effortlessly. If you look closer at geese, you will find that there is an order, a science, in the way they position themselves when they fly. They fly in a "V" formation.

There is a scientific reason for this. Researchers found that as each goose flaps its wings, an updraft is created for the bird immediately following. Studies show that this "V" formation adds at least 71 percent greater power than if the birds had flown alone.

There really is benefit in doing things together. The real beauty is not just the strength that they gain from each other in the "V" formation, but the lead geese on both sides of the "V" are encouraged by each other. The noise being made are geese cheering for the leaders to keep the faith and keep the speed. When the lead geese are tired, they rotate to the back of the "V" and others will assume the point position. It is truly remarkable to observe.

If one goose becomes ill or is shot and falls out of formation, two other geese will follow and nurture the goose hopefully to health. If the goose dies, they will form a new "V" formation and attempt to catch the original group. Wouldn't it be nice if people would function the same way?

Eagle Selection

There really is a science to selecting a mate. It is unfortunate that many humans do a better job selecting their cars, clothes, and houses than selecting a mate. If you look at the animal kingdom, there is an order on how to select a mate. Eagles are fascinating, not only in the way they fly, but in the way they select a mate.

If you observe closely, you will see the female eagle drop a tree branch near an eagle that she thinks has potential. If the male eagle is able to pick up the branch and return it to the female eagle then she knows there is potential. She will then drop a heavier weight branch to see if the male eagle can manage.

There is a reason for this. If the male eagle can pick up this branch, it indicates the male eagle is also able to pick up a baby eagle and return it back to the mother.

The selection process is not complete. The female eagle will then drop a heavier branch to see if the male eagle can pick this up and return it to her. If the male eagle can do this, she knows he can carry her. She wants to know "will you be there for me?" Maybe sisters need to watch female eagles the next time they are looking for a mate, "waiting to exhale," and trying to get their "grove back."

An Arabian Colt

(Inspired by Terri McFaddin)

Of all the horses that God made, there is probably no more elegant animal than an Arabian colt. It is truly a royal animal, but not at birth. Few would know at birth the uniqueness of the Arabian colt. At birth this horse may be worth only $1,000, but if nurtured, developed, and tested, it can command hundreds of thousands of dollars.

There are ways to develop this colt to reach God's full potential. Those master trainers know the best test is over the Saharan Desert. Many colts are not able to endure the terrain and heat. The period between infancy and two years is the critical time to develop their full potential. If the Arabian colt can endure the heat and harshness of the Saharan Desert, they are valuable.

This parallels the many Africans who were tested as they lay in the dungeons and went through "the door of no return." A far greater number died on the slave ships, not only killing themselves but also their babies. Many jumped over the ship or refused to eat. Unfortunately, a greater number died on the plantation. Those who survived the worse holocaust known to man had to be very special.

The River and the Desert

(Inspired by Ayi Kwei Armah)

Have you noticed that the river is always giving, always flowing, and always moving? Have you noticed that oftentimes the waves will take the water from the lake, river, stream, or ocean and flow toward the shore to nurture the soil and provide nutrients for trees, grass, and plants? Have you noticed that the ocean seems to be endless and is home for so many animals including the whales? It is expansive and it reminds me of God. When you look at the water, you can't see the beginning or the end.

Let's now look at the desert. The desert seems to stand still, always taking, always absorbing, and always destroying. It is unfortunate that there are some people who are like the desert. It is the nature of water to give. It is the nature of water to flow. It is the nature of the desert to take. Water represents life and the desert represents death. If the water continues to flow toward the desert, will there be any more water? The challenge for five billion people of color living in the world is, how can they live with people who act like the desert?

Stretch Me

(Inspired by Reverend Frederick Haynes III)

Freddie Haynes had an unusual revelation. It did not come from a deacon, minister, nor from his wife. It came from an unusual product, a little tiny rubber band. He had a conversation with a rubber band and said, "talk to me, rubber band." The rubber band said, "Freddie, I get better the more you use me. Right now I am very small, but when the load gets heavy, when the package gets longer, when the object becomes wider, I expand and get better."

"Stretch me, Freddie. Use me. I may be little to you now, but if you use me, and give me your problems, watch me grow, Freddie. See how wide I get? See how long I become? I get better the more you use me. Right now I am a new rubber band, but look at my older friends who have been used. They have held problems for a long time."

Isn't that just like God? The more you lean on Him and the more you put your problems on Him, He becomes wider, taller, and stronger.

A Welfare Mentality

(Inspired by Aesop)

The canary walked proudly as a peacock and possessed beautiful feathers. A man noticed the uniqueness of the bird and offered a worm for a feather. The canary thought this was a win-win proposition. He had plenty of feathers and now he would not have to work for food.

The man returned each morning and gave the canary a worm in exchange for a feather. The canary enjoyed his worm every morning. Unfortunately, one day the man did not appear. The canary was hungry and did not know what to do. He had become fat, featherless, and could not fly.

Ironically, welfare has done the same for many people. They do not want or know how to work. They have become fat, lazy, and expect someone to take care of them.

PART 9

SOME OF THE GREATEST BIBLICAL STORIES

That I will pour out my Spirit on all flesh.
Your sons and daughters will prophesy.
Your old men will dream dreams. Your
young men shall see visions.

Let Go

There was once a famous mountain climber who felt that there was no mountain that he could not climb. This one particular day he had climbed to the peak of the mountain. On his way down, however, he stumbled and almost fell, but at the last minute, he was able to secure a ragged rock on the side of the mountain. He was still more than 1,000 feet up. He didn't know what to do. No one was there with him—at least that is what he thought.

After about an hour of holding on, the man finally said, "God, please save me." A voice said, "I will." The man said, "Who are you?" The voice replied, "The Lord." The man said, "I'm glad you are here. Please save me." The voice said, "Before I save you, do you believe in me?" The mountain climber responded, "You know I believe in you. I go to church when I am not climbing mountains, I give some of my money when I am there, I put my Bible in my backpack, why would you ask me a question like that?" The voice responded, "But do you really believe I am who I am?" The mountain climber was becoming anxious and said, "You know I believe you. I would give my life for you."

The Lord said, "That is what I was waiting to hear. Now let go of the branch." The mountain climber looked in amazement and began to stutter, "You mean you want me to let go of this branch?" And the Lord said, "You said you believe in me, you said you would give your life for me. Then let go of the branch." There was silence for several minutes and then the mountain climber yelled, "Is there anybody else up there?"

The Least of These

'For I was hungry and you gave Me food; I was thirsty and you gave Me drink; I was a stranger and you took Me in.'

'I was naked and you clothed Me; I was sick and you visited Me; I was in prison and you came to Me.'

Then the righteous will answer Him, saying, 'Lord, when did we see You hungry and feed You, or thirsty and give You drink?'

'When did we see You a stranger and take You in, or naked and clothe You?'

'Or when did we see You sick, or in prison, and come to You?'

And the King will answer and say to them, 'Assuredly, I say to you, inasmuch as you did it to one of the least of these My brethren, you did it to Me.'

Matthew 25:35-40

Be honest. When you see the homeless, the lost, begging on the streets, do you see Jesus? How would you feel if someone sat next to you in church who had not bathed? How many checks could you miss before you were homeless?

Once upon a time in East Africa in the country of Tanzania there was a king. He was becoming older and was looking for an heir. Everyone thought that he would appoint one of his children or grandchildren, but he was not pleased with their maturity and wisdom. He felt that there was someone in the larger community that would be better. An announcement was made throughout the country. There were two major qualifications. The new king must love God and love his fellow man. Anyone in the country that thought they could fulfill those qualifications was encouraged to have a meeting with the king.

Twenty-five miles outside of a major city Dar es Salaam a young man began walking to meet with the king. He knew he loved God and people and felt confident he would be selected as the king. He was well dressed and had bathed himself very well. Everyone in his community felt he looked like a king. Halfway through his journey, he met a beggar by the side of the road. The beggar was tattered and torn and was begging for money for food and clothes. The young man knew that if he stopped and took care of this beggar it would delay his visit to the king. He also knew that he could not afford to give this beggar any of his clothes for he needed them to make a good impression. A small voice kept saying, "What you do unto the least of these you also do unto me." He couldn't shake the voice, even though he tried several times. He gave the beggar half of his money and gave him his shirt and his shoes. The young man continued on to meet the king, but now he only had pants and was barefoot.

He reached the palace late that evening. The guards looked him up and down and said, "Go away. The king does not want to see you. You are not dressed like a king and do not smell like a king." As the man began to turn away, the beggar was walking toward the palace. The guards could not believe it and they said, "Your highness, what happened to you?" The young man looked at the king, or should I say he looked at the beggar. No, he looked at the king. No, he looked at the beggar. The king saw the young man's confusion and told his guards, "Open up the gates and let us both in for I have found the new king." When they went into the palace the young man asked the king, "Why did you do that?" The king said, "This was the only way for me to be sure. People can say anything in the palace, but what they do outside illustrates their true character."

I was hungry and you formed a humanities club to discuss my hunger.

Thank you.

I was imprisoned and you crept off quietly to your chapel to pray for my release.

Nice.

I was naked and in your mind you debated the morality of my appearance.

What good did that do?

I was sick and you knelt and thanked God for your health.

But I needed you.

I was homeless and you preached to me of the shelter of the love of God.

I wish you'd taken me home

I was lonely and you left me alone to pray for me.

Why didn't you stay?

You seem so holy, so close to God; but I'm still very hungry, lonely, cold, and still in pain.

Does it matter?

Anonymous

You can Choose the Sin, but not the Consequence

A father pounded a nail in the barn door every time the boy did something wrong. Soon there were many nails. Then one day the boy accepted Christ as his Savior and began living for Him. The father took his son to the barn and pulled out every nail from the door to impress upon him the gift of forgiveness. "That is what it means to have all of your sins forgiven," he said. "They are gone forever." The boy was deeply impressed. Then, looking at the door he asked, "But father, how can I get rid of the holes?" "I am sorry," said the father, "but they will remain." All sin carries a price tag. Its consequences may range from minor to major, but the bill always comes due. Somebody always pays. If someone has sex out of marriage, they chose the sin, but the consequence could be divorce, pregnancy, sexually transmitted disease, a physical fight, and sometimes death. You can chose the sin, but not the consequence.

God Doesn't Wear a Uniform

It was a beautiful day along Lake Michigan. A wonderful day for sailing. Numerous boats were out on the lake. People were taking in the sun. A sailor went out in his boat. He was experienced, his boat was in excellent condition, and he wanted to avoid the congestion from boats closer to shore. Unfortunately, a sudden storm appeared. He remained confident in his skills and knew he would be okay. The storm worsened, the sun disappeared, clouds came, and darkness enveloped the lake.

A larger boat drew near and an officer called out, "Do you need any help? Do you want to tie your boat to ours? We are returning back to the shore." The man hollered back, "Thank you but I am okay. God will take care of me." The crew aboard looked at him very perplexingly, but went on to shore. Several minutes later the Coast Guard drew near and said, "The storm is worsening. Everyone needs to return back to shore." The man told the Coast Guard that he was fine. He had been in the Navy for 20 years, felt confident, and God provides. The Coast Guard thought this was strange, but they were not going to argue with someone in the middle of a storm. An hour later a helicopter flew over the boat, and the pilot pointed toward the shore. The sailor waved and said, "I'm okay, God provides."

Unfortunately, hours later the boat capsized and the sailor died. He was furious and when he went to Heaven he said to the angels, "Let me speak to God immediately." The angels looked perplexed and said to themselves, "He should be glad that he made it up here." The angels ushered the man in to talk to God and the man hollered out to God, "I thought you loved me? I thought you said you would never leave me nor forsake me?" God said, "I do love you and I never have left you or forsaken you." The man told God, "But you lied to me. You did leave me, you did forsake me. I died and you could have saved me." God bit his lip trying to hold back his frustration and said, "I sent someone to rescue you three times. I sent a yacht, the Coast Guard, and a helicopter. Whom do you think sent them?"

Justice and Mercy

(Inspired by Reverend Jeremiah Wright, Jr.)

Today was the big day. This Friday it was finally going to be resolved. The big debate was going to take place. We were finally going to determine which was more important, Justice or Mercy. Who was right? Very similar to the debate between Malcolm and Martin. Do we believe an eye for an eye, a tooth for a tooth, a life for a life? Today we were going to resolve this. Who was right? The debate would be held on Friday at twelve-o'clock. Both parties would provide evidence to support their position. Martin had been trying to convince Malcolm for years that if you continue to believe an eye for an eye and a tooth for a tooth and a life for a life, you will have blind people, toothless people, and dead people.

As expected, when Friday came, at twelve o'clock noon, Justice was present. He was always on time. He believed in order. Everything had a place and everything should be in its place. If you believe in the law, if you do things the way they are supposed to be done, there will never be a need for forgiveness and mercy. These are signs of weakness. When you operate from a standpoint of strength and justice there is no need for such wimpish activity as mercy. As per usual Mercy was late. Justice tried to appeal to the Judge that he should win because the agreement was Friday at noon. Justice provided his evidence. He cited example after example, court case after court case on how things work better when there is order and logic. The Judge said he would give Mercy until three-o'clock before making the final decision. Justice was furious. He knew he was right and Mercy was stalling. Two hours went by and Justice said, "Could you at least realize after two hours it is obvious that Mercy is not going to show? She is afraid of what will happen and has chosen not to appear." The Judge overruled and said, "We will wait until three-o'clock."

Finally, at two fifty-five Mercy appeared. While Justice was neatly dressed in a dapper designer suit, Mercy looked like she had been through the ringer. She was tattered and torn. The first thing Justice said to Mercy was, "Where have you been?" Mercy shook her head and said, "You can't imagine what I have been through. First, I had to walk Moses over the Red Sea, Pharaoh was chasing behind him with his army, and they were trying to kill Moses and the Israelites. It was tough for awhile, but I provided a carpet for them and Pharaoh's army drowned." Justice shook his head and said, "That is no excuse for being late. You should have let the Hebrews die. They probably had done something wrong anyway or Pharaoh would not have been chasing them."

Mercy went on, "Your honor, I apologize for being late, but Daniel got caught in the lion's den. They wanted him to bow down and acknowledge their god and Daniel was not going to compromise. I had to step in and put my hand in the lion's mouth to protect Daniel. Your honor, it didn't stop there. When I thought that I was going to make it, unfortunately, the Hebrew boys had the same problem. They too were not going to bow down to a foreign god and they were placed in a fiery furnace. It was hot. The Hebrew boys had no reason being there and so I had to step in and that is why unfortunately I look the way I do."

Justice was flabbergasted and said, "They had to have done something wrong or the king would not have placed them in a fiery furnace. People don't do things just to be doing them." The Judge overruled and said, "Continue on, Mercy." She said, "I had to break up a fight. There was going to be warfare between this huge giant named Goliath and this little boy named David who only had some rocks and a sling shot. Your honor, you could see that this was not fair, even Justice should understand that." Justice said, "I thought it was fair. David shouldn't have been there in the first place. Someone else should have fought Goliath." Mercy continued, "So I had to step in and give David some extra fire power with his sling shot and his five rocks."

"Then came the problem with Paul and Silas. They were to be executed at midnight. They were innocent. They had done nothing wrong except praise His name. Your honor, when I was almost here, Mary and Martha called and said their brother, Lazarus, was dead. They were on my case because they said if I had shown earlier, Lazarus would not have died. I had to move the rock. It smelled very bad. I apologize, but that is why I smell the way that I do, but Lazarus is alive."

"Then some Roman soldiers nailed me to the cross, pierced me on the side, and that is why you see blood stains. Before I left I told them 'Father forgive them for they know not what they do.'" Justice was irate. He looked at the Judge and said, "Are you going to believe this nonsense?" The Judge looked at Mercy and then looked at Justice and said, "Yes. It is finished." Justice walked out the door in rage. Mercy and the Judge hugged each other and Mercy said to the Judge, "Father, into your hands I commit my spirit."

A Wise Decision

1st Kings 3:16-28

What happens when someone commits the perfect crime? When no one is present except the criminal, the victim, and the Lord? What happens when DNA results are not conclusive or are unavailable? Would O.J. Simpson have been acquitted had he not had the financial resources and a jury of his peers? Three police officers beat Rodney King senseless and their argument was he resisted arrest because he moved while they hit him. They were tried and acquitted in Simi Valley. Remember all the White men who lynched and bombed Black people who were never convicted.

It was a very tough case. Two women presented themselves before King Solomon. They were fighting over a child. One mother said, "He is my baby." The other mother said, "No, King, he is my baby." One mother said, "She lost her baby and stole mine."

What would you do? It was the perfect crime. No one was there except the victim, the criminal, and the Lord. This case had no lawyers. Money was not be a factor. This case had no jury, therefore, Simi Valley or South Central Los Angeles would not be an issue. When God asked Solomon, "What is it that you want from me?" Solomon asked for wisdom. "Had you been the judge over this case what would have been your decision?" Solomon looked both mothers in the eye and with the wisdom of God told them, "Cut the baby in two. This way we will have justice. Since only the two of you were present, we will give each of you half a child." The mother who was lying accepted the offer. The mother who was telling the truth screamed to Solomon and said "No! She can have the child." At that point Solomon knew who was telling the truth.

A Daddy's Love

2nd Samuel 18:33

I can still hear David crying out, "Oh my son, Absalom. My son, my son, Absalom. If only I had died in your place." I can see David, I feel his tears. I can see David jumping out in front of danger to save his child. David had gone through so much. He killed Uriah, committed adultery with Bathsheba, and the child they conceived died while David fasted and prayed.

I love to see fathers play with their children in the park. I adore observing them holding their babies and walking down the street. It soothes my soul to see daddies at PTA meetings asking questions. I like watching children sit on their father's lap asking question after question and fathers patiently answering. I urge the media to portray fathers in a much better light. Oh, how nice it would be if every once in a while the news would show fathers doing the right thing.

We Will Be Back

Genesis 22

Did I miss something in the story? Am I unable to follow the plot? Didn't God ask Abraham to sacrifice their only son Isaac? The child he waited 90 years to receive and loved so much?

At the beginning of the story, God asked Abraham to sacrifice his son and Abraham agrees. In the middle of the story Abraham says to his staff, "Stay here with the donkey and we will go worship and we will come back." Now I am a little slow on math, but if Abraham agreed to sacrifice his son and tells his men to stay where they are, and he and the boy are going to worship and both will come back, how is Abraham going to be obedient to God and both return?

The plot thickens. Isaac becomes confused. Isaac realizes there is going to be a sacrifice. He observes the fire and wood, but where is the animal for a burnt offering? Isaac and I are confused and Abraham doesn't understand subtraction problems. Why did Abraham say, "We will be back?" He walked by faith and not by sight. Abraham remembered the covenant God promised him and his descendants. Who or what is your Isaac? What is it that you value so much if the Lord asked you to sacrifice it you would have second thoughts?

Satan Knows Our Weakness

Remember when Adam was all by himself? God was pleased on every day except when he saw Adam was lonely. Adam needed a help mate. So God took woman out of Adam's ribs, and when Adam saw her he hollered out, "WHOOOOOOO MAAAAN!" and has been excited about women ever since. God saw how excited man was about women. Women are very beautiful in the eyes of men.

Unfortunately, Satan saw how much men valued and loved looking at women. He saw how men could be so foolish about women. Satan got four of our best. David was after God's own heart yet it was not enough when Satan set him up with Bathsheba. Solomon asked for God's wisdom, but it was not enough when Satan set Solomon up with more than 300 women who manipulated him to even give up his relationship with God. Samson had almost all of God's strength, but it was not enough when Satan set him up with Delila who kept asking, "What makes you so strong?"

Bill Clinton was one of our youngest Presidents, entered the Oval Office at the age of 46, easily won his second term, had one of the highest approval ratings in the history of the country, and Satan set him with Monica Lewinsky. Satan got four of our best, David, Solomon, Samson, and Clinton.

Fortunately, he didn't get Joseph. Was it because Joseph was a dreamer? Was it because Joseph was ugly? Was it because Satan didn't try Joseph? What did Joseph do that David, Solomon, Samson, and Clinton did not do? Joseph did not have David's heart, Solomon's wisdom, Samson's strength, or Clinton's Presidency, but Joseph knew there are some places you should not go or stay. There are some situations that cannot be discussed or negotiated. There are some situations you need to get the hell out of as soon as you can.

What Do You See?

Numbers 13

It is amazing how some people see rain while others see sunshine. Some see happiness while others view sadness. Others see opportunity while some see disappointment. Remember the story about the baseball team that was losing fourteen to nothing? At the end of the inning, they were asked how they felt and a player responded, "There is no need to worry, we have not batted yet."

Moses sent twelve spies to go into Canaan, the promised land, and bring back a report. Ten of the twelve, the majority, came back and said, "There we saw giants and we were like grasshoppers in our own sight and so we were in their sight." Some African Americans view themselves as grasshoppers and view Whites as giants. Some African Americans believe giants have colder water, sweeter lemonade, smarter doctors and lawyers, and better businesses.

Remember Moses sent out twelve, not ten. There were two, Joshua and Caleb, the minority, who had a different report. Caleb told Moses, "We went to the land where you sent us. It truly flows with milk and honey. Let us go up at once and take possession for we are well able to overcome it." Why did Joshua and Caleb see things differently? What did they see that the others did not? Why is it that the majority thought they were grasshoppers? Whose report will you believe? Are you a grasshopper or a giant?

But If Not

Daniel 3

Shadrach, Meshach, and Abed Nego said to the king, "Oh, Nebuchadnezzar, we have no need to answer. If that is the case, our God whom we serve is able to deliver us from the burning fiery furnace and He will deliver us from your hand o' king. *But if not* let it be known to you o' king that we do not serve your gods nor will we worship the gold image which you have set up." Can you imagine the audacity of these three Hebrew boys? They not only talked back to the king, but told him they were not going to bow down and worship their god.

Could you imagine if you were in the military and were a captive and tortured by the enemy, and they told you it would stop if you simply acknowledged their god? Would you go along and do as the Romans do? What makes it more amazing is that the Hebrew boys not only said they would not bow down, but they did not know if they would be saved in the furnace or be allowed to enter Heaven. If everybody believed that when they gave their life to Christ there would be no trials and tribulations, people would use God as a blessing machine.

These Hebrew boys told Nebuchadnezzar that God would either save them in the furnace or in eternity. They knew God was going to save them. God looked down on his three children, and tears came down his eyes when he heard them say *"but if not."* He knew he had to come down to save his children.

In Heaven, on the throne, God asked his deacon board, "How long would it take for you to get down to the fiery furnace to save them?" The deacons said, "We could be there in five minutes," and God said that was not fast enough. He went to his ministers and asked, "How long would it take for you to get down to the fiery furnace and save them?" The ministers quickly said, "Three minutes." God again shook his head and said, "That's not fast enough." He then called on his angels and asked, "How long would it take you to save them?" The angels said "We could be there in a minute." God gritted his teeth and said, "That's not fast enough." Jesus hollered up and said, "I'm already there. I am in the furnace with them."

Heaven or Hell?

Three teenage boys, Michael, Marcus, and Matthew, did almost everything together. They lived on the same block, attended the same school, played ball, listened to rap, and talked about girls. They were almost inseparable and many people thought they were brothers.

Unfortunately, one day they were in a fatal car accident. All three died. Michael noticed Marcus and Matthew were rising toward a door marked "Heaven." Sadly, he was sinking to a door marked "Hell." Michael hollered to Marcus and Matthew, "Why am I sinking? Why are you rising? Can you take me with you?" Marcus and Matthew looked sad. Michael pleaded and screamed, "I thought we did everything together! Why didn't you tell me?"

EPILOGUE

The Miracle Under the Hood

(contributed by Howard Conister)

Two teenage sisters, Cindy and Karen, had been shopping in a suburban mall. When they were ready to go home, it was dark. Their car was one of the few remaining in the parking lot. They were nervous and hoping some other customers would come along so that they could all walk out together. They were aware of the current crime wave in area shopping malls and remembered Dad's warnings, "Don't stay too late." Cindy shifted her packages, pushed open the door, and walked as fast as she could with Karen following, both looking from side to side. They just made it.

Cindy shoved the key into the door lock, got in, reached across to open Karen's door and then they both heard the sound of running feet behind them. They turned to look and panicked. Racing toward their car were two ominous looking men. One of them shouted, "We got you. You're not going anywhere." Karen jumped in and they both locked their doors just in time. With shaking hands, Cindy turned the ignition switch. Nothing. She tried again and again but still nothing. Click. Silence. No power.

The men were ready to smash a window. The girls knew there were scant seconds of safety left so they joined hands and prayed. "Dear God," Karen pleaded, "Give us a miracle in the name of Jesus." Cindy turned the key and the engine roared to life and they raced out of the lot. The girls cried all of the way home, shocked and relieved. They screeched into the driveway, pulled the car into the garage, burst into the house, spilling out their story to Mom and Dad.

"You're safe, thank God, that is the main thing. But don't do it again," Dad said. Then their father frowned. "It's strange. That car has never failed to start. I'll just check it out I'll take a look at it now." In the garage he raised the hood and in one stunned glance he realized Who had brought his daughters home safely that night. There was no battery in the car!

And God Said No

I asked God to take away my pride and God said "No."

He said it was not for Him to take away but for me to give up.

I asked God to make my handicapped child whole and God said "No."

He said "The spirit is whole, the body is only temporary."

I asked God to give happiness and God said "No."

He said He gives blessings, happiness is up to me.

I asked God to spare me pain and God said "No."

He said "Suffering draws you apart from worldly cares and brings you closer to Me."

I asked God if He loves me and God said "Yes."

He gave me His only son who died for me that I would be in Heaven someday because I believe.

I asked God to help me love others as much as He loves me and God said "Ah! Finally, you have the idea!"

Anonymous

Notes and Credits

Stories included in this book were collected over the past decade. Reasonable care has been taken to trace original ownership. Some stories have been retold when there was no clue of the story's origin. If I have overlooked giving proper credit to anyone, please contact African American Images and corrections will be made prior to additional editions. Listed below are acknowledgments and credits.

What Makes You So Strong?, Jeremiah Wright Jr., Judson Press, Valley Forge, Pennsylvania.

Africans Who Shaped Our Faith, Jeremiah Wright Jr., Urban Ministries, Chicago, Illinois.

Good News! Sermons For African American Families, Jeremiah Wright Jr., Judson Press, Valley Forge, Pennsylvania.

Reverend Jeremiah Wright Jr., Trinity United Church of Christ, Chicago, Illinois, (Sermon Series).

Reverend Frederick Haynes III, Friendship West Baptist Church, Dallas, Texas, (Sermon Series).

Reverend Ozzie Smith, Covenant United Church of Christ, South Holland, Illinois.

"God Made Me Beautiful" audio cassette, Terri McFaddin, Pasadena, California.

Aesop Fables, Penguin, New York, New York.

Voices For the Future, Bob Law, African American Images, Chicago, Illinois.

Two Thousand Seasons, Ayi Kwei Armah, Third World Press, Chicago, Illinois.

Reverend Howard Conister, Beverly Hills Baptist Church of Dallas, Dallas, Texas.

The Treasure excerpted from *More Stories for the Heart*, © 1997 by Alice Gray and reprinted by permission of Multnomah Publishers, Inc.